more easy

Windows 98

See it done

Do it yourself

que®

Copyright© 1998 by Que® Corporation

International Standard Book Number: 0-7897-1740-9

Library of Congress Catalog Card Number: 98-85583

01 00 99 98   4 3 2 1

Interpretation of the printing code: the rightmost double-digit number is the year of the book's printing; the rightmost single-digit, the number of the book's printing. For example, a printing code of 98-1 shows that the first printing of the book occurred in 1998.

Composed in Baker Signet by Macmillan Computer Publishing

Printed in the United States of America

President:	Richard K. Swadley
Publisher:	Dean Miller
Executive Editor:	Christopher Will
Director of Editorial Services:	Carla Hall
Managing Editor:	Sarah Kearns
Indexing Manager:	Ginny Bess

About the Author

Joe Kraynak has been writing and editing computer books and other technical material for over 10 years. His long list of computer books includes *The Complete Idiot's Guide to PCs*, *The Big Basics Book of Windows 98*, *10 Minute Guide to Excel*, *Easy Internet*, and *Windows 95 Cheat Sheet*. Joe graduated from Purdue University in 1984 with a Master's degree in English, a Bachelor's degree in Philosophy and Creative Writing, and a strong commitment to making computers and software easily accessible to the average user.

Dedication

To my parents, John and Adeline Kraynak. Thanks for everything!

Acknowledgments

Several people contributed their talent and hard work to making this a successful book. Special thanks to Chris Will for choosing me to write this book and to Kate Welsh for guiding the content of this book and keeping it focused on new users. And thanks to Brian-Kent Proffitt, technical reviewer, for making sure the information in this book is accurate and timely. Finally, the Macmillan design and production team merits a round of applause for transforming a collection of electronic files into such an attractive, bound book.

Acquisitions Editor
Christopher Will

Development Editor
Kate Shoup Welsh

Project Editor
Kate Shoup Welsh

Copy Editor
Kate Shoup Welsh

Indexer
Chris Barrick

Technical Reviewer
Brian-Kent Proffitt

Editorial Coordinator
Mandie Rowell

Editorial Assistants
Jen Chisholm, Lori Morgan, Tracy Williams

Cover Designers
Anne Jones, Karen Ruggles

Book Designer
Jean Bisesi

Illustrator
Bruce Dean

Copy Writer
Bill Meiners

Production Team Supervisor
Tricia Flodder

Production Designer
Trina Wurst

Proofreader
Jeanne Clark

How to Use This Book

It's as Easy as 1-2-3

Each part of this book is made up of a series of short, instructional lessons, designed to help you understand basic information that you need to get the most out of your computer hardware and software.

1 Each step is fully illustrated to show you how it looks onscreen.

Click: Click the left mouse button once.

Double-click: Click the left mouse button twice in rapid succession.

 Tips and **Warnings** give you a heads-up for any extra information you may need while working through the task.

Right-click: Click the right mouse button once.

2 Each task includes a series of quick, easy steps designed to guide you through the procedure.

Pointer Arrow: Highlights an item on the screen you need to point to or focus on in the step or task.

Selection: Highlights the area onscreen discussed in the step or task.

Click & Type: Click once where indicated and begin typing to enter your text or data.

Drag

Drop

How to Drag: Point to the starting place or object. Hold down the mouse button (right or left per instructions), move the mouse to the new location, then release the button.

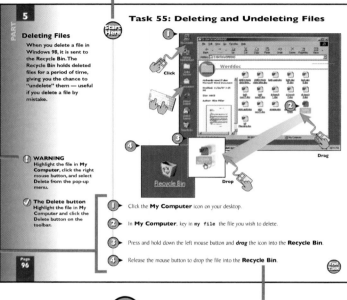

Task 55: Deleting and Undeleting Files

Deleting Files
When you delete a file in Windows 98, it is sent to the Recycle Bin. The Recycle Bin holds deleted files for a period of time, giving you the chance to "undelete" them — useful if you delete a file by mistake.

WARNING Highlight the file in **My Computer**, click the right mouse button, and select **Delete** from the pop-up menu.

The Delete button Highlight the file in My Computer and click the Delete button on the toolbar.

Page 96

1 Click the **My Computer** icon on your desktop.

2 In **My Computer**, key in `my file` the file you wish to delete.

3 Press and hold down the left mouse button and **drag** the icon into the **Recycle Bin**.

4 Release the mouse button to drop the file into the **Recycle Bin**.

3 Items that you select or click in menus, dialog boxes, tabs, and windows are shown in **bold**. Information you type is in a `special font`. Items that are defined in the glossary are *italic*.

Next Step: If you see this symbol, it means the task you're working on continues on the next page.

End Task: Task is complete.

Introduction to More Easy Windows 98

You know the Windows 98 basics. You can install and run applications, create and print documents, manage files and folders, play Solitaire, and maybe even tinker with the Windows desktop. In short, you have mastered the Windows interface, and you can accomplish your daily tasks in Windows 98.

However, you need to dig a little deeper than the Windows desktop to find the stash of new and improved features. With a little exploration, you'll find that Windows offers an enhanced desktop, a new Maintenance wizard for optimizing your system, a drive converter for reclaiming hard disk space, and dozens of additional tools for Internet access, portable computing, networking, and troubleshooting.

More Easy Windows 98 acts as your guide to the advanced features of Windows 98. It doesn't rehash what you already know or waste time bringing you up to speed. Instead, *More Easy Windows 98* dives right in, showing you just how to optimize your system, configure Windows, make the most of your notebook PC and network, and even solve problems when your system acts up. This book also throws in a good chunk of timesaving tips and shortcuts that can transform you from novice to master in a matter of minutes.

You can read this book from cover to cover or use it as a reference when you encounter a feature (or a problem) that you just don't know how to approach. Either way, *More Easy Windows 98* lets you see how it's done and shows you how to do it yourself.

PART 1

Optimizing Windows 98

You might think that your system is running at its peak performance, but do you know for sure? Are errant files cluttering your hard disk? Is Windows set up to take advantage of your speedy hard drive? Is your printer printing at its optimum speed? Can your CD-ROM read discs any faster?

In this part, you learn the answers to these questions and many more as you examine your system and use the Windows 98 tools to optimize its components. Here, you will learn how to clear useless files from your disk drive, rearrange files so your system can find them more quickly, reduce the time it takes Windows to "wake up" in the morning, remove fonts and Windows components you don't use, and much more. By the end of this part, you'll know for sure that your system is finely tuned and in tip-top condition.

Tasks

Windows 98 includes a new tool, the Maintenance wizard, that can clear useless files from your hard disk, make Windows start faster, defragment files on your hard disk to make it run faster, and scan for and fix disk errors. You can also use the Maintenance wizard to schedule these system tune-ups regularly, ensuring that your system is always running its fastest.

✓ Schedule your system tune-ups for times when your system is typically on but when you are not actively using it. The tune-up utilities can slow down your system as they are working.

⚠ **WARNING**
Some programs that automatically run when you start Windows may protect your system against viruses or offer features that you do not want to disable.

Task 1: Running the Windows Maintenance Wizard

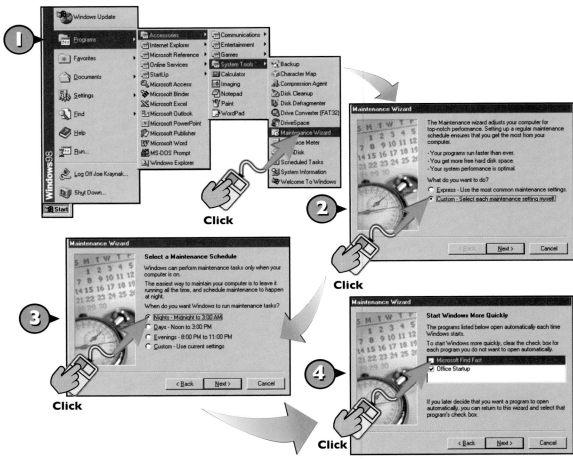

1 ▶ Choose **Start**, **Programs**, **Accessories**, **System Tools**, **Maintenance Wizard**.

2 ▶ Click **Custom** and click **Next**.

3 ▶ Choose **Nights**, **Days**, or **Evenings** and click **Next**.

4 ▶ To have Windows start faster, remove the check mark next to any programs that run on startup. Click **Next**.

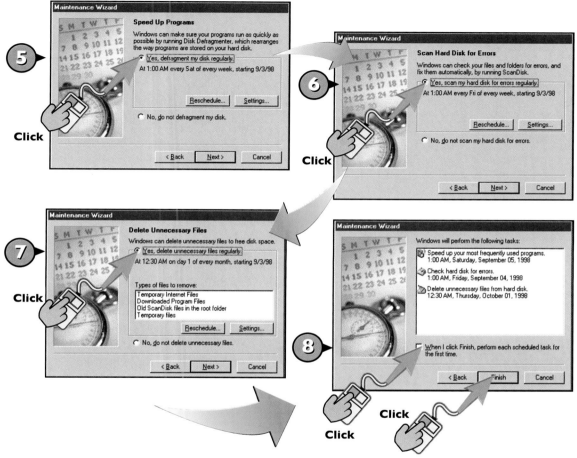

The Windows Maintenance wizard actually runs several utilities that are part of Windows 98, including ScanDisk (**Start, Programs, Accessories, System Tools, ScanDisk**), Disk Defragmenter (see Task 5, "Defragmenting Your Hard Disk Drive") and Disk Cleanup (see Task 2, "Reclaiming Disk Space with Disk Cleanup").

When scheduling Windows to run a system utility, click the **Reschedule** button to specify a time. Click the **Settings** button to tell the utility how to do its job.

WARNING
Windows considers files in the Recycle Bin to be unnecessary. You might want to click the **Settings** button in step 7 and turn off the option for deleting files from the Recycle Bin. See Task 3, "Configuring the Recycle Bin to Save Disk Space."

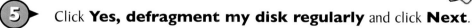

5 ▶ Click **Yes, defragment my disk regularly** and click **Next**.

6 ▶ Click **Yes, scan my hard disk for errors regularly** and click **Next**.

7 ▶ Click **Yes, delete unnecessary files regularly** and click **Next**.

8 ▶ Click **When I click Finish, perform each scheduled task for the first time** (if desired) and click **Finish**.

Task 2: Reclaiming Disk Space with Disk Cleanup

Start Here

As you create and edit files, delete folders and files, install programs, and explore the Internet, Windows and your applications store temporary files in various folders on your hard disk. To reclaim this disk space, you can use Disk Cleanup to find and delete these files.

✓ To quickly run Disk Cleanup, right-click a drive icon in My Computer and choose **Properties**. Click the **Disk Cleanup** button.

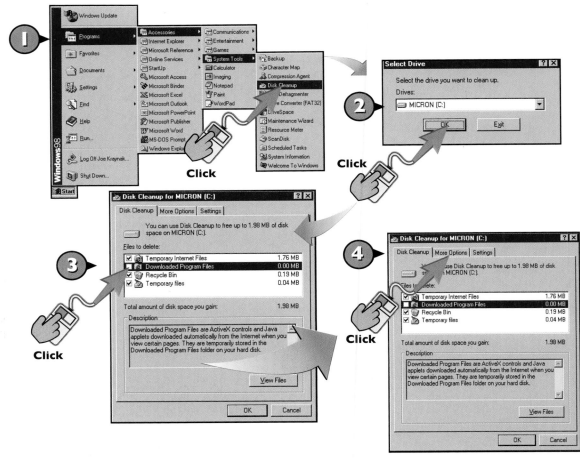

Click

Click

Click

Click

1 ▶ Choose **Start**, **Programs**, **Accessories**, **System Tools**, **Disk Cleanup**.

2 ▶ Choose the letter of the drive you want to clean up and then click **OK**.

3 ▶ Click to place a check mark in the box for each type of file you want Disk Cleanup to remove from your system.

4 ▶ To free additional disk space, click the **More Options** tab.

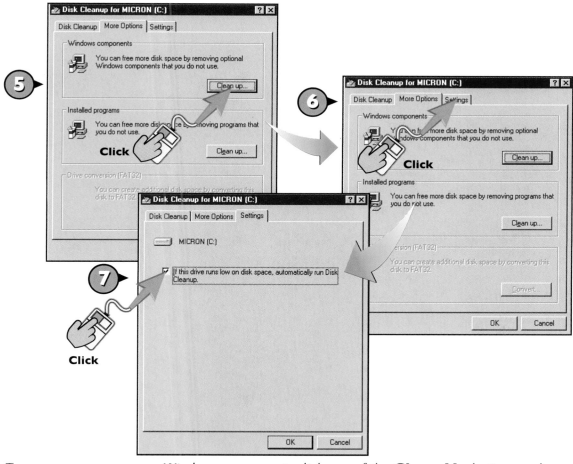

The More Options tab allows you to use other Windows features to remove applications and Windows components you do not use and to convert your hard disk drive to FAT32. For information on removing Windows components, see Task 11, "Removing Windows Components." For details about FAT32, see Task 4, "Converting Your Hard Drive to FAT32."

5 ▶ To remove a program or a Windows component, click one of the **Clean Up** buttons and follow the instructions.

6 ▶ Click the **Settings** tab.

7 ▶ Make sure the **If this drive runs low on disk space, automatically run Disk Cleanup** check box is selected. Click **OK**.

 Not all programs add their names to the list of programs you can uninstall. If an installed program is not on the list, check the program's folder in My Computer for an Uninstall or Remove icon.

As you delete files, you rarely give a thought that those files are sitting in the Recycle Bin, still taking up valuable hard disk space. Although you can permanently remove the files by emptying the Recycle Bin, you can have this done automatically by telling the Recycle Bin to use less disk space.

Task 3: Configuring the Recycle Bin to Save Disk Space

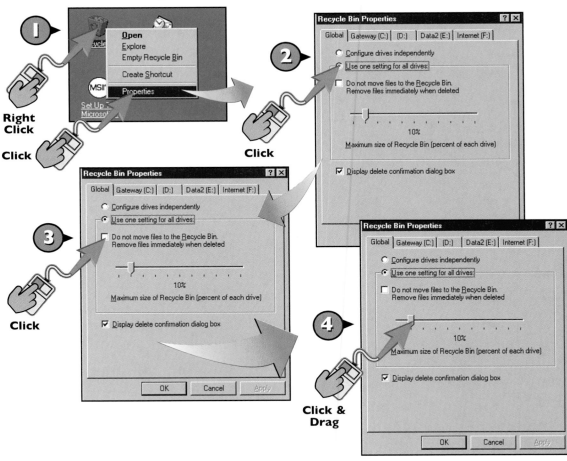

To bypass the Recycle Bin and permanently delete selected files, hold down the **Shift** key while clicking the **Delete** button or press **Shift+Delete**.

 Right-click the **Recycle Bin** icon and click **Properties**, or **Alt+click** the **Recycle Bin** icon.

 If you have multiple drives, you can choose **Use one setting for all drives**.

 To have folders and files deleted permanently when you delete them, choose **Do not move files to the Recycle Bin**.

 To specify the percentage of drive space to use for the Recycle Bin, drag the slider to the left or right.

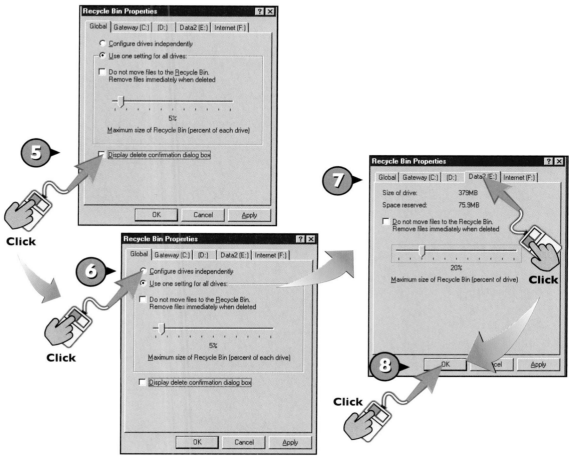

5 To prevent a warning from appearing when you delete files, click **Display delete confirmation dialog box** to turn it off.

6 If you have two or more hard disks, you can choose **Configure drives independently**.

7 Click the tab for the drive whose settings you want to change, and enter your preferences.

8 Click **OK**.

⚠ WARNING
Do not turn on the option for bypassing the Recycle Bin and turn off the option for displaying the confirmation dialog box. This disables both of the fail-safe systems, making it very risky to delete files.

End Task

Drive Converter can safely reconfigure the way your hard drive stores files to increase its storage capacity. It transforms your drive from FAT16 (which stores files in 32KB chunks, no matter how small the file) to FAT32 (which stores files in 4KB chunks). This can reclaim a large amount of wasted space.

✓ Drive Converter can optimize large hard disk drives (over 500MB), but may not increase storage space on smaller hard drives.

⚠ **WARNING**
Before converting your hard drive to FAT32, you should back up your files.

Task 4: Converting Your Hard Drive to FAT32

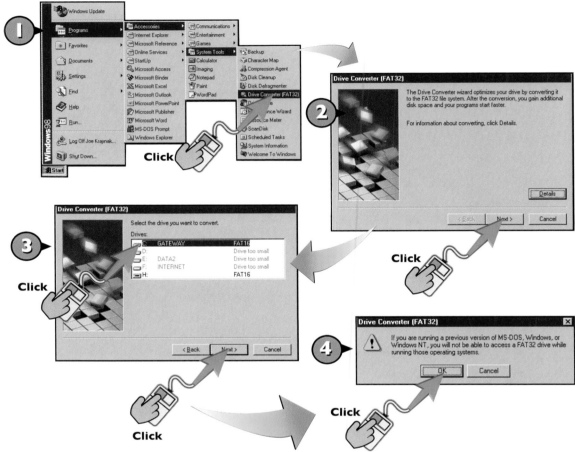

① Choose **Start**, **Programs**, **Accessories**, **System Tools**, **Drive Converter (FAT32)**.

② Read the introduction to Drive Converter and click **Next**.

③ Click the drive you want to convert from FAT16 to FAT32 and click **Next**.

④ Read the warning that older operating systems cannot access FAT32 drives and click **OK** if you wish to proceed.

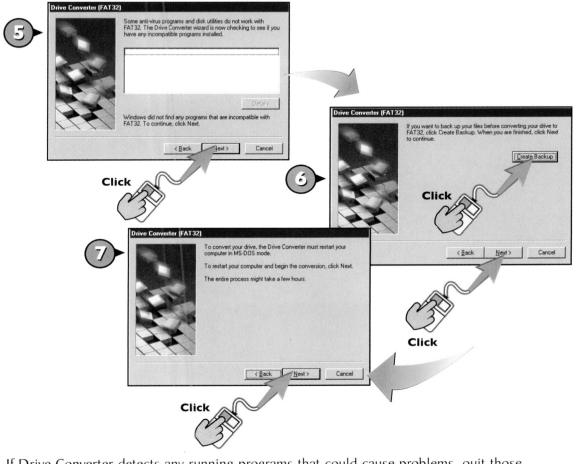

With disk drives over 500MB, older operating systems (using **FAT16**) would use 32KB of hard drive space to store even a small file of 2KB, leaving 30KB of wasted space.

5 ▸ If Drive Converter detects any running programs that could cause problems, quit those programs. Click **Next**.

6 ▸ If you have not recently backed up files, click **Create Backup** and follow the instructions. Click **Next**.

7 ▸ Click **Next** to restart your computer and allow Drive Converter to convert your hard disk drive to FAT32.

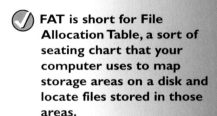 **FAT is short for File Allocation Table, a sort of seating chart that your computer uses to map storage areas on a disk and locate files stored in those areas.**

As you save and delete files, your files become fragmented. That is, parts of each file are stored on areas of the disk that are located far away from other storage areas. This slows down your disk and makes it more likely that your files can be lost or damaged. Defragmenter rewrites the files, placing the parts of each file on neighboring storage areas.

 Defragmenter can also place program files at the beginning of your disk, so they run faster.

 Click the **Settings** button to enter your preferences. Make sure **Rearrange program files** is checked.

Task 5: Defragmenting Your Hard Disk Drive

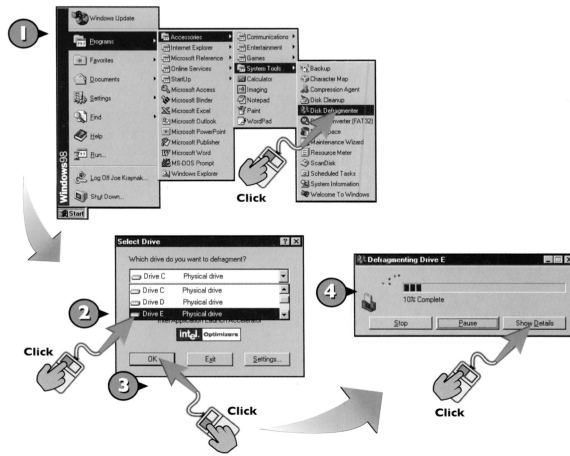

Choose **Start**, **Programs**, **Accessories**, **System Tools**, **Disk Defragmenter**.

Open the drop-down list and choose the disk drive you want to defragment.

Click **OK**.

If desired, click **Show Details** to see Defragmenter in action.

Task 6: Speeding Up Your Hard Disk Drive

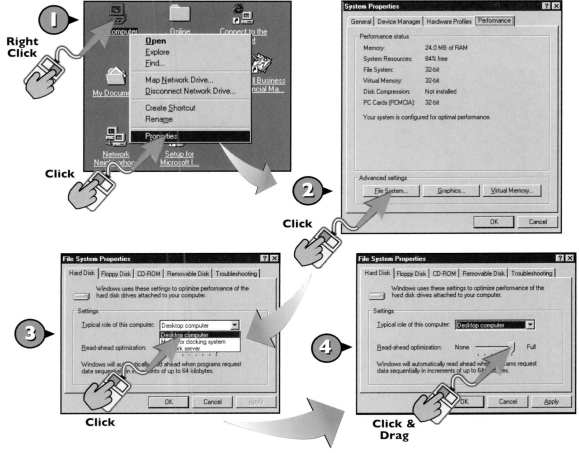

Right Click

Click

Click

Click

Click & Drag

Compared to **RAM** (memory), your hard disk is slow. To increase the speed at which **Windows** can read from the disk, you can increase the amount of **RAM** used for the *read-ahead buffer*. This allows your system to read more than what is immediately needed from the disk and store it in **RAM**, where Windows can quickly access it.

1 ▶ Right-click **My Computer** and choose **Properties**.

2 ▶ On the **Performance** tab, click the **File System** button.

3 ▶ Open the **Typical role of this computer** drop-down list and choose the type of computer you have.

4 ▶ Drag the **Read-ahead optimization** slider to specify the amount of RAM to use. Click **OK**.

✓ Alt+click the **My Computer** icon to display the **System Properties** dialog box.

⚠ **WARNING**
If your system has less than 16MB of RAM, you may want to *decrease* the amount of **RAM** used for the read-ahead buffer.

Task 7: Speeding Up Your CD-ROM Drive

Even a fast **CD-ROM** drive is slower than **RAM** (memory) or your hard disk drive. To speed it up, you can have Windows read more of the disk than is immediately needed and store the data in **RAM**, where it is easily accessible.

(✓) If you rarely use your CD-ROM drive, and your system has less than 32MB of RAM, decrease the supplemental cache size to give Windows and your applications more RAM.

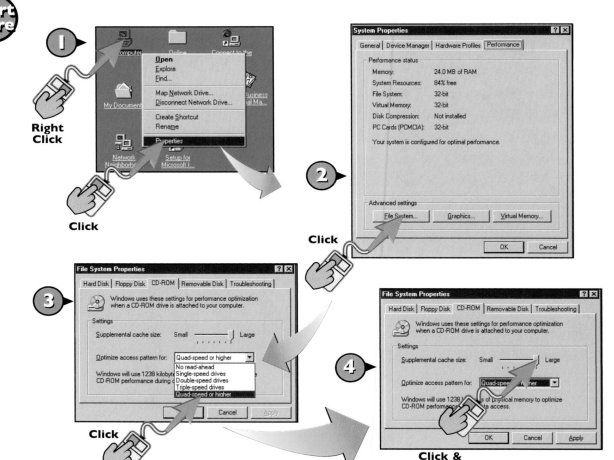

Start Here

Right Click

Click

Click

Click

Click & Drag

➀► Right-click **My Computer** and choose **Properties**.

➁► On the **Performance** tab, click the **File System** button.

➂► On the **CD-ROM** tab, open the **Optimize access pattern for** drop-down list and choose the speed of your CD-ROM drive.

➃► Drag the **Supplemental cache size** slider to specify the amount of RAM to use. Click **OK**.

End Task

Task 8: Adjusting the Virtual Memory Settings

Start Here

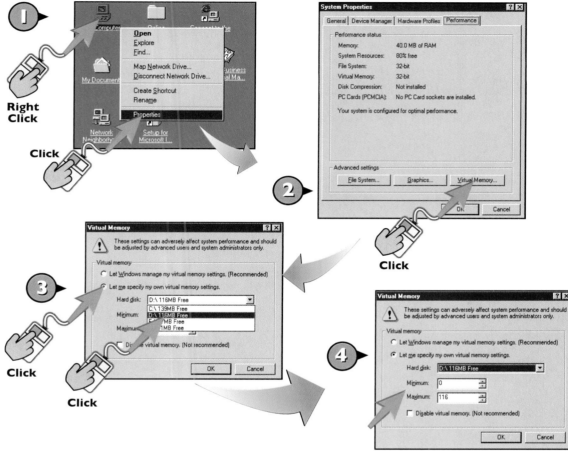

Right Click

Click

Click

Click

Click

Click

Click

Windows and your applications typically require more **RAM** (memory) than is installed on your computer. To make up for any memory shortfall, Windows uses your hard disk drive as *virtual memory*. You can adjust the virtual memory settings to increase or decrease the amount of disk space Windows uses.

⚠ WARNING
It's usually best to let Windows manage virtual memory. However, if you have two hard drives, you should choose the faster drive.

✓ If you have multiple drives, select the drive you want to use, click **OK**, click **Virtual Memory** again, and choose the option to let Windows manage virtual memory.

1 ▶ Right-click **My Computer** and choose **Properties**.

2 ▶ On the **Performance** tab, click the **Virtual Memory** button.

3 ▶ Choose **Let me specify my own virtual memory settings** and choose the fastest drive with the most free space.

4 ▶ Enter any other preferences and click **OK**.

End Task

Page
15

When you install a printer, the printer uses the default settings, which typically favor quality over speed. For faster printing, you can decrease the print quality for both graphics and text and turn on the spool settings, so Windows can print while you work in other programs.

✓ Run your computer's BIOS setup program when you turn it on (see Tasks 17, "Running Your Computer's BIOS Setup," 18, "Navigating the BIOS Setup Screen," and 20, "Checking Your Printer Port Setting"), and make sure the printer port setting is correct for your printer, as specified in the printer manual.

⊘ **WARNING**
The options in the **Printer Properties** dialog box vary depending on the printer.

Task 9: Optimizing Your Printer's Performance

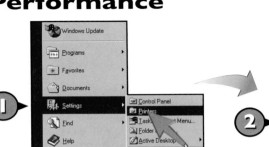

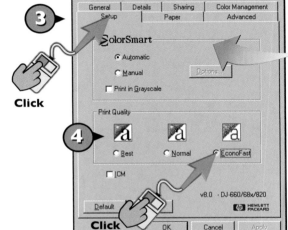

1 ▶ Choose **Start**, **Settings**, **Printers**.

2 ▶ Right-click your printer and choose **Properties**.

3 ▶ Click the tab that contains the print quality settings.

4 ▶ Enter your preferences for print quality, color, and speed.

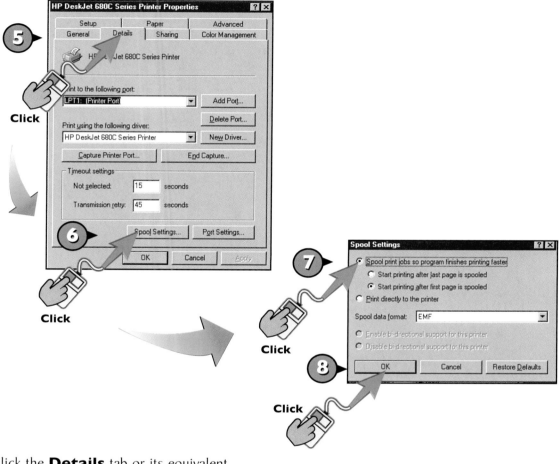

To allow you to work while Windows prints, Windows stores printing instructions temporarily on your hard disk and then *spools* those instructions to your printer.

Click the **Details** tab or its equivalent.

Click the **Spool Settings** button.

Make sure **Spool print jobs so program finishes printing faster** is selected and enter any additional preferences.

Click **OK** to return to the **Printer Properties** dialog box and then click **OK** to save your settings.

End Task

Microsoft continues to perfect Windows 98, adding new device drivers and improving its performance. To ensure that you have the latest version of Windows, you should check for and install updates on a regular basis. Windows Update can automatically download and install updates from Microsoft's Web site.

Task 10: Upgrading Windows with Windows Update

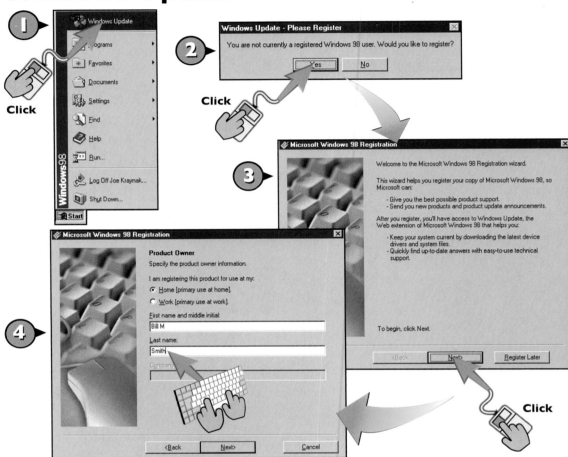

Click

Click

Click

①▶ Choose **Start**, **Windows Update**.

②▶ Internet Explorer runs and connects you to the **Windows Update** page. When prompted to register, click **Yes**.

③▶ When the Registration wizard appears, click **Next**.

④▶ Follow the onscreen instructions and complete the forms to register your copy of Windows 98.

Next Step

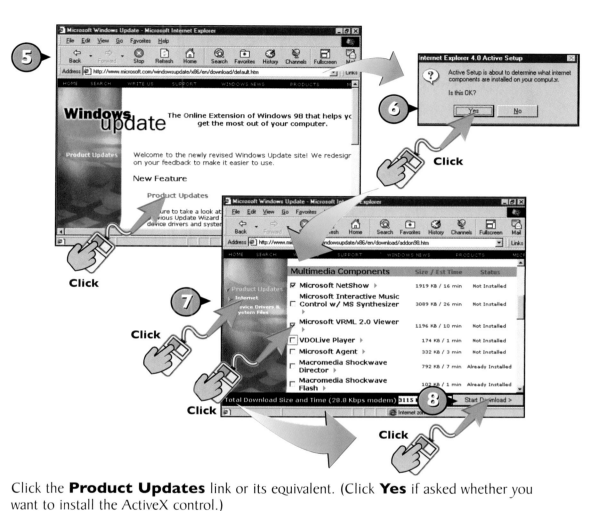

You can also use **Windows Update** to download updated device drivers (for running your monitor, display adapter, printer, and so on) as explained in Part 8, Task 4, "Installing Updated Device Drivers."

Schedule **Windows Update** to run every month or every other month. Part 7, Task 2, "Scheduling Tasks to Run Automatically," shows you just what to do.

WARNING
Microsoft is constantly updating **Windows Update**, so the steps may vary. You must be flexible when working on the Web.

5 ▸ Click the **Product Updates** link or its equivalent. (Click **Yes** if asked whether you want to install the ActiveX control.)

6 ▸ When the **Active Setup** dialog box asks for permission to check your system, click **Yes**.

7 ▸ Choose the desired category of Windows components and click the check box next to each one you want installed.

8 ▸ Click the **Start Download** button in the lower-right corner of the screen.

Task 11: Removing Windows Components

When you installed Windows, the installation program may have installed Windows components that you don't plan on using. To reclaim disk space occupied by those components, you can remove them.

⚠ WARNING

Before removing a component, read its description, so you know what it does. You don't want to remove Dial-Up Networking if you use the Internet features.

✓ You can use Add/Remove Programs to install additional components, as well.

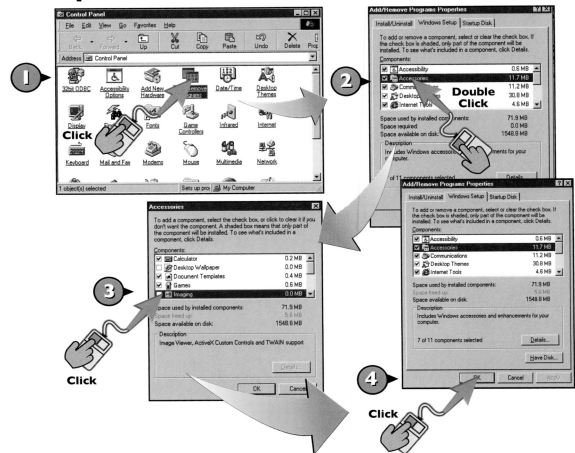

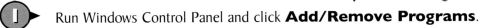

1 ▶ Run Windows Control Panel and click **Add/Remove Programs**.

2 ▶ On the **Windows Setup** tab, double-click the desired component category to view a list of available components.

3 ▶ To remove a component, click the check box next to its name to remove the check mark. Click **OK**.

4 ▶ You can repeat these steps to remove additional components. Click **OK** when you are done.

Task 12: Removing Fonts

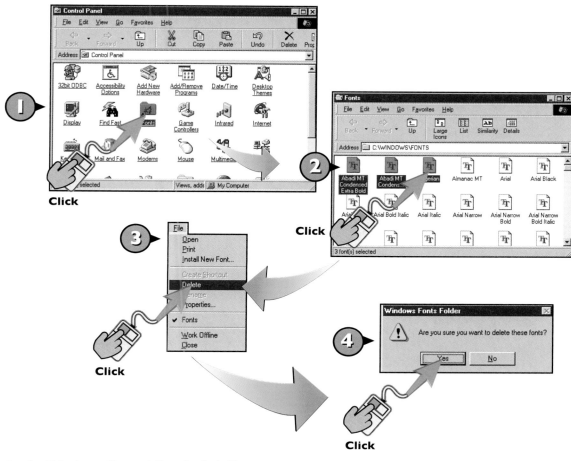

Click

Click

Click

Click

Windows and most applications you install come with their own fonts that are placed on your hard disk during installation. These fonts can take up a good chunk of disk space. To reclaim that space, consider removing similar fonts or fonts you don't use.

⚠ **WARNING**
Do not remove any font named **System** or **MS Sans Serif**. These fonts are used to display menu and dialog box option names.

✅ Click the **Similarity** button in the toolbar to group similar fonts.

✅ Double-click a font's name to preview it.

① In the Windows Control Panel, click **Fonts**.

② Click the name of the font you want to delete. (You can select additional fonts by **Ctrl+clicking** their names.)

③ Choose **File**, **Delete**.

④ When prompted to confirm the deletion, click **Yes**.

Not only does Windows 98 help you manage your daily computer tasks, it can also help trim your electric bills and increase the life span of your computer. Its power-management features can automatically shut down your monitor and hard drive when you're not using them and wake them up when you're ready to work.

Task 13: Adjusting the Power-Management Settings

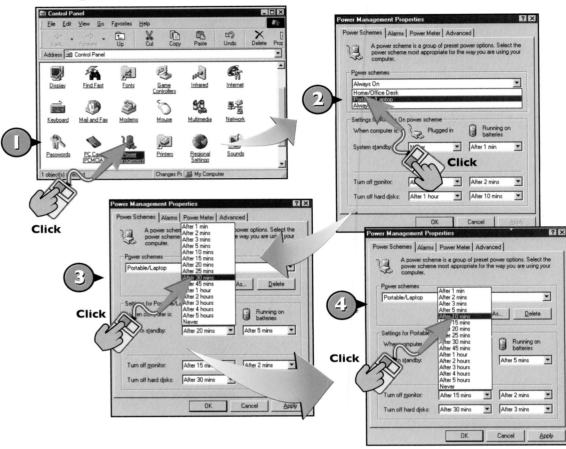

✓ The options in the **Power Management** window depend on the type of system you have. A notebook PC includes options for conserving battery power.

① In the Windows Control Panel, click the **Power Management** icon.

② Open the **Power schemes** drop-down list and choose the desired option: **Home/Office Desk**, **Portable/Laptop**, or **Always On**.

③ Open the **System standby** drop-down list (if available) and choose the period of inactivity before Windows places your system in Standby mode.

④ Open the **Turn off monitor** drop-down list and choose the period of inactivity before Windows turns off the monitor.

Next Step

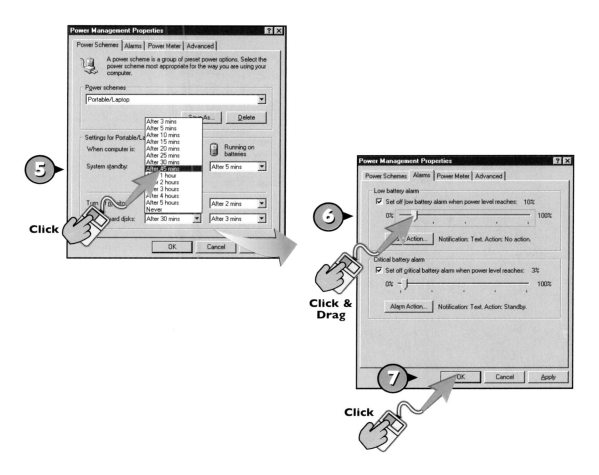

On a notebook PC, you can also enter settings that tell Windows to sound an alarm (or display a message) when the battery power dips below a certain level. You can then save your work before shutting down your computer and replacing or recharging the battery.

WARNING
Windows' power-management features may conflict with your system's built-in power-saving features. You may need to disable the Windows features by choosing **Always On**.

To change the way Windows notifies you of low battery power, click one of the **Alarm Action** buttons and enter your preferences.

5 Open the **Turn off hard disks** drop-down list and choose the desired period of inactivity before turning off the hard drives.

6 In the **Alarms** tab, drag the sliders to the desired settings if you are configuring settings for a notebook PC.

7 Click **OK** to save your settings.

Task 14: Setting Up Windows for Multiple Users

If you need to share your computer with coworkers or family members, you don't want the other users reconfiguring your Windows desktop or messing with special settings you've entered. To keep everyone happy, you should set up Windows for multiple users.

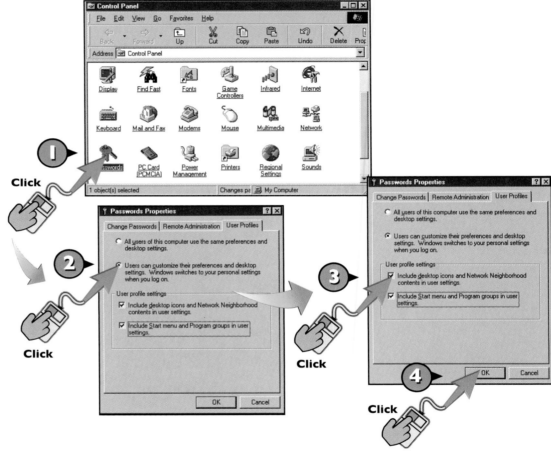

Click

Click

Click

Click

Start Here

WARNING

Your Windows password does not prevent other people from using the computer. It merely prevents them from signing on as you and changing your configuration settings.

I ▶ In the Windows Control Panel, click the **Passwords** icon.

2 ▶ Click the **User Profiles** tab and choose **Users can customize their preferences...**.

3 ▶ Under **User profile settings**, make sure both options are checked.

4 ▶ Click **OK**.

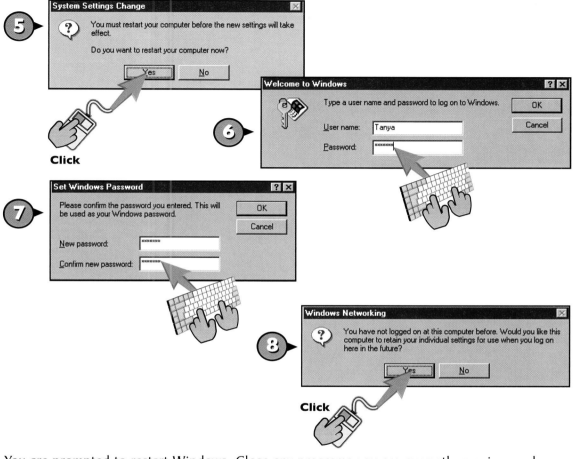

Click

After setting up Windows for multiple users, Windows displays a logon dialog box on startup, prompting you (or another user) for your name and password. You must enter the requested information and click OK to start using Windows.

Click

✅ **Passwords are optional. If all the people using the computer trust each other, you can log on as unique users without passwords. Just leave the Password text box blank.**

✅ **When you are done working and are ready to turn over the computer to another user, choose Start, Log Off so another user can log on.**

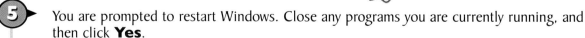

5 ▸ You are prompted to restart Windows. Close any programs you are currently running, and then click **Yes**.

6 ▸ When prompted, enter your username and password, and click **OK**.

7 ▸ When prompted to confirm, type your password again and click **OK**.

8 ▸ The first time you log on, Windows asks if you want your configuration settings to be saved. Click **Yes**.

End Task

Task 15: Using Different Hardware Profiles

You can connect different devices to your computer depending on what you plan on doing. For example, you might want to connect a mouse or a larger monitor to your notebook PC when you're working at home. To help Windows determine which devices you are using and prevent hardware conflicts, you create a *hardware profile*.

When you install a new device, Windows runs the Add New Hardware wizard on startup and leads you through the process of setting up the device.

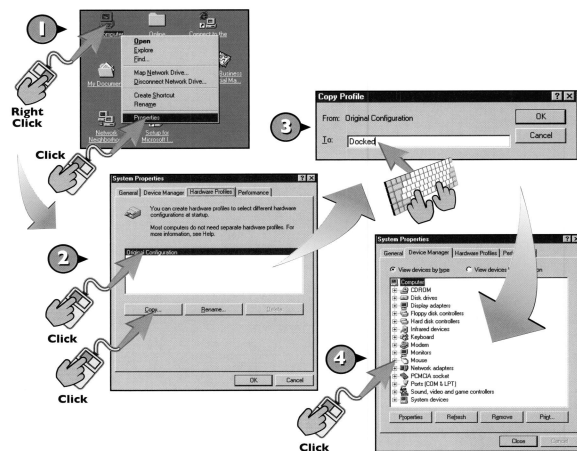

Start Here

Right Click

Click

Click

Click

Click

Click

> Right-click **My Computer** and choose **Properties**.

> On the **Hardware Profiles** tab, click **Original Configuration** and click **Copy**.

> Type a name for the new configuration and click **OK**.

> Click the **Device Manager** tab and click the plus sign next to a device type that you want to disable.

Next Step

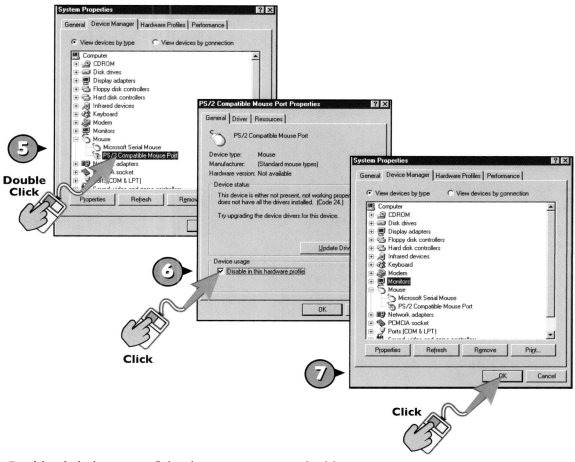

In a hardware profile, you can disable devices that are not connected to the computer and enable devices that are connected. When Windows starts, it automatically loads the hardware profile for the installed devices or prompts you to choose a profile.

Double Click

Click

Click

5 ► Double-click the name of the device you want to disable.

6 ► Click **Disable in this hardware profile**, and click **OK**.

7 ► Repeat the steps to disable any additional hardware, and then click **OK**.

 Hardware profiles are especially useful if you have a notebook PC and a docking station or port replicator. You can boot with one profile when not docked and another for when you dock your PC.

End Task

Hillingdon Libraries

Task 16: Finding Additional Software on the Windows CD

The Windows 98 CD contains all sorts of goodies that you can't get at using Add/Remove Programs, including additional software, demos of Microsoft products, audio and video clips, clip art, and an electronic version of the Windows Resource Kit.

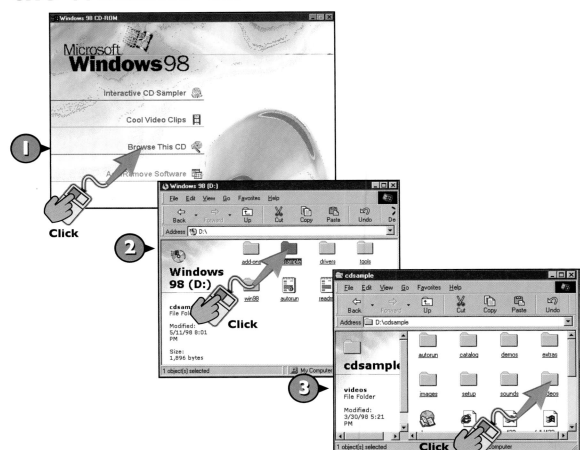

Start Here

Click

Click

Click

✓ The Windows Resource Kit includes valuable information for when you're ready to tackle advanced Windows 98 tasks and deal with high-tech issues.

1 Insert the Windows CD into your computer's CD-ROM drive and click the **Browse This CD** link.

2 Click the **cdsample** folder to check out some interesting objects that have not been installed on your hard disk.

3 Click the **demos**, **graphics**, **sounds**, or **videos** link (in this example, I've clicked videos).

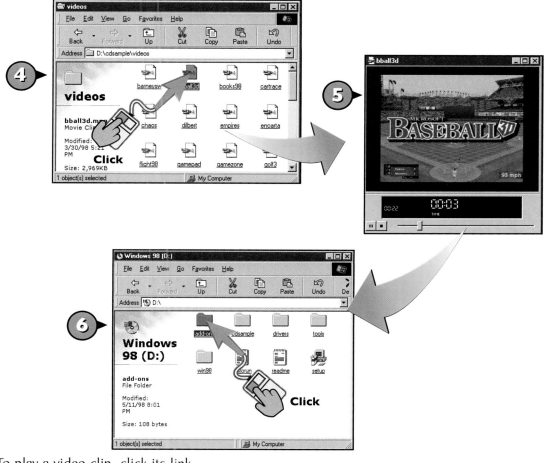

Check out the catalog folder for Web links to Microsoft products, demos for online demonstrations of products, extras for free trial versions, images for clip art that you can use on your own Web pages, sounds for additional audio clips, and videos to check out some video clips.

4 ▸ To play a video clip, click its link.

5 ▸ The Windows movie player opens the file and starts playing the clip.

6 ▸ Explore other folders on the Windows CD by clicking their icons.

Task 17: Running Your Computer's BIOS Setup

Your computer's BIOS (basic input/output system) acts as traffic cop for all of your computer hardware. Although the BIOS is not directly related to Windows 98, you can often adjust the BIOS settings to improve the performance of Windows.

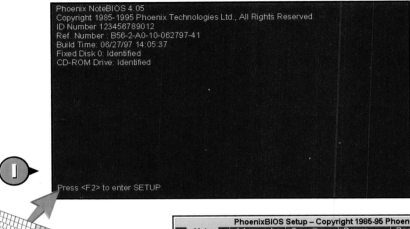

```
Phoenix NoteBIOS 4.05
Copyright 1985-1995 Phoenix Technologies Ltd., All Rights Reserved.
ID Number 123456789012
Ref. Number : B56-2-A0-10-062797-41
Build Time: 06/27/97 14:05:37
Fixed Disk 0: Identified
CD-ROM Drive: Identified




Press <F2> to enter SETUP
```

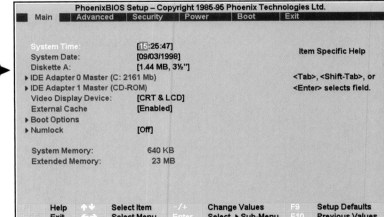

```
                    PhoenixBIOS Setup – Copyright 1985-95 Phoenix Technologies Ltd.
   Main    Advanced    Security    Power    Boot    Exit

   System Time:          [15:25:47]                        Item Specific Help
   System Date:          [09/03/1998]
   Diskette A:           [1.44 MB, 3½"]
 ▶ IDE Adapter 0 Master (C: 2161 Mb)                    <Tab>, <Shift-Tab>, or
 ▶ IDE Adapter 1 Master (CD-ROM)                        <Enter> selects field.
   Video Display Device:  [CRT & LCD]
   External Cache:        [Enabled]
 ▶ Boot Options
 ▶ Numlock              [Off]

   System Memory:         640 KB
   Extended Memory:       23 MB



      Help    ↑↓   Select Item   -/+    Change Values   F9   Setup Defaults
      Exit    ←→   Select Menu  Enter   Select ▶ Sub-Menu F10  Previous Values
```

 WARNING

Keep a written log of any BIOS setting you change and the change you made, so you can change it back if you encounter problems. Do not change any settings you don't understand.

 In most cases, before Windows starts, the BIOS displays the keys you must press to access the BIOS setup program.

1 ▶ Start your computer, and press the specified keystroke(s) to run the BIOS setup (refer to your computer manual).

2 ▶ The BIOS Setup screen appears. This screen and the available options differ depending on the BIOS.

Task 18: Navigating the BIOS Setup Screen

Start Here

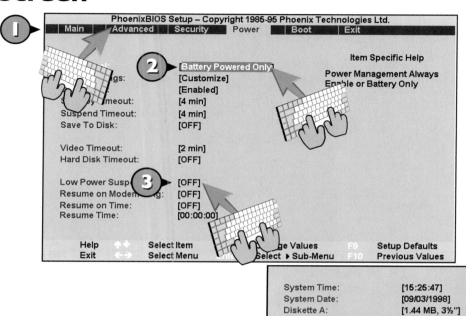

PhoenixBIOS Setup – Copyright 1985-95 Phoenix Technologies Ltd.

| Main | Advanced | Security | Power | Boot | Exit |

Item Specific Help

[Battery Powered Only]
...gs: [Customize]
              [Enabled]
S... ...meout: [4 min]
Suspend Timeout: [4 min]
Save To Disk: [OFF]

Video Timeout: [2 min]
Hard Disk Timeout: [OFF]

Low Power Susp... [OFF]
Resume on Modem...g: [OFF]
Resume on Time: [OFF]
Resume Time: [00:00:00]

Power Management Always
Enable or Battery Only

| Help | ↑↓ | Select Item | ...ge Values | F9 | Setup Defaults |
| Exit | ←→ | Select Menu | ...elect ▶ Sub-Menu | F10 | Previous Values |

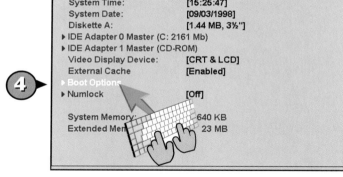

System Time: [15:25:47]
System Date: [09/03/1998]
Diskette A: [1.44 MB, 3½"]
▶ IDE Adapter 0 Master (C: 2161 Mb)
▶ IDE Adapter 1 Master (CD-ROM)
Video Display Device: [CRT & LCD]
External Cache   [Enabled]
▶ Boot Options
▶ Numlock   [Off]

System Memory: 640 KB
Extended Mem...   23 MB

Because the **BIOS** setup runs before your computer runs the mouse driver, you must use your keyboard to navigate the **BIOS Setup** screen and enter your changes. This can be a little tricky if you're not accustomed to it.

---

1 Press the left or right arrow key to change from one menu of options to another.

2 Use the down and up arrow keys to highlight an option you want to check or change.

3 Press the plus or minus key to change a value displayed in brackets, for instance to change **[Off]** to **[On]**.

4 Highlight an option preceded by an arrow and press **Enter** to view its submenu.

 Press F1 for help.

End Task

Task 19: Bypassing the Floppy Drive on Startup

Some computers are set up to first look to the floppy disk drive for boot instructions on startup. You can reduce the time it takes your system to start by having your computer look to the hard drive first.

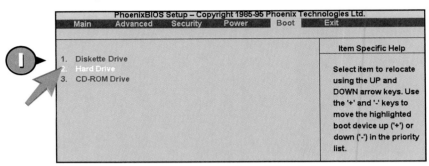

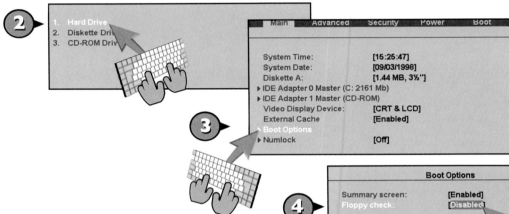

If your system crashes and you have to boot with your **Windows Emergency Recovery Disk**, you may have to change this setting back before booting.

1 On the Boot menu, highlight the option for the disk on which Windows is installed (typically **Hard Drive**).

2 Press the plus key to move this option to the top of the list.

3 On the **Main** menu, highlight **Boot Options** and press **Enter**.

4 Highlight **Floppy Check [Enabled]** and press the plus key to change the setting to **[Disabled]**.

Task 20: Checking Your Printer Port Setting

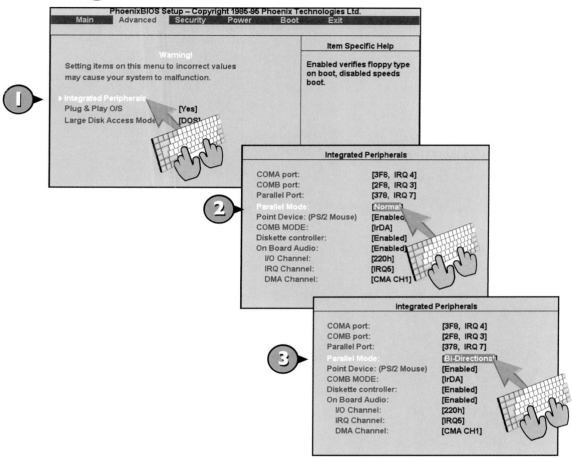

Most newer printers support bi-directional printing, which enables the printer to print nearly twice as fast. However, your computer's parallel port must be set in bi-directional mode, which you do through the **BIOS** setup.

 On the **Advanced** menu, highlight **Integrated Peripherals** and press **Enter**.

 Highlight the **Parallel Mode** option.

 Press the plus or minus key to change the setting to **[Bi-Directional]** or **[ECP]** (Extended Capabilities Port).

 Make sure you connect your bi-directional printer to your system unit's printer port with a bi-directional cable.

Task 21: Checking Your Computer's Power-Saving Features

Although Windows 98 comes with a power-management utility, your computer may have built-in power-conservation features. Frequently, these features may conflict with Windows power-management settings or with other software. You can adjust or disable these settings in the BIOS Setup.

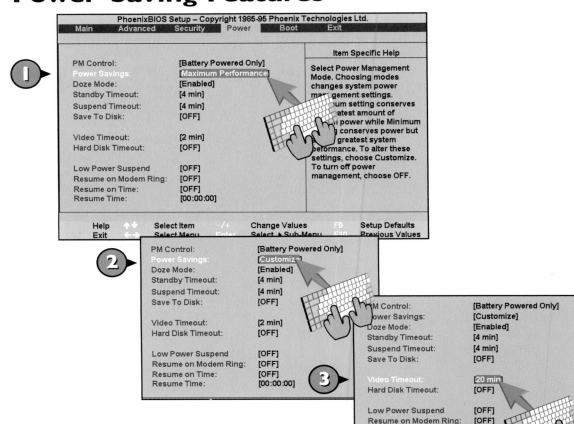

```
PhoenixBIOS Setup – Copyright 1985-95 Phoenix Technologies Ltd.
  Main      Advanced     Security     Power      Boot       Exit

                                                    Item Specific Help
  PM Control:          [Battery Powered Only]
  Power Savings:       [Maximum Performance]     Select Power Management
  Doze Mode:           [Enabled]                 Mode. Choosing modes
  Standby Timeout:     [4 min]                   changes system power
  Suspend Timeout:     [4 min]                   management settings.
  Save To Disk:        [OFF]                      um setting conserves
                                                   atest amount of
  Video Timeout:       [2 min]                     power while Minimum
  Hard Disk Timeout:   [OFF]                       conserves power but
                                                   greatest system
  Low Power Suspend    [OFF]                  performance. To alter these
  Resume on Modem Ring: [OFF]                 settings, choose Customize.
  Resume on Time:      [OFF]                  To turn off power
  Resume Time:         [00:00:00]             management, choose OFF.

      Help    ↑↓   Select Item    -/+    Change Values    F9    Setup Defaults
      Exit    ←→   Select Menu    Enter  Select ▶ Sub-Menu F10  Previous Values
```

```
  PM Control:          [Battery Powered Only]
  Power Savings:       [Customize]
  Doze Mode:           [Enabled]
  Standby Timeout:     [4 min]
  Suspend Timeout:     [4 min]
  Save To Disk:        [OFF]

  Video Timeout:       [2 min]
  Hard Disk Timeout:   [OFF]

  Low Power Suspend    [OFF]
  Resume on Modem Ring: [OFF]
  Resume on Time:      [OFF]
  Resume Time:         [00:00:00]
```

```
  PM Control:          [Battery Powered Only]
  Power Savings:       [Customize]
  Doze Mode:           [Enabled]
  Standby Timeout:     [4 min]
  Suspend Timeout:     [4 min]
  Save To Disk:        [OFF]

  Video Timeout:       [20 min]
  Hard Disk Timeout:   [OFF]

  Low Power Suspend    [OFF]
  Resume on Modem Ring: [OFF]
  Resume on Time:      [OFF]
  Resume Time:         [00:00:00]
```

✓ If your computer has problems waking up from sleep mode, try disabling the power-saving features to see if that corrects the problem.

1 ▸ On the **Power** menu, highlight the **Power Savings** option.

2 ▸ Press the plus key to cycle through the available options. (To disable the power-saving features, choose **[Off]**.)

3 ▸ If you chose **[Customize]** in step 2, you can enter settings for powering down the display and hard disk.

End
Task

Task 22: Saving Your Changes

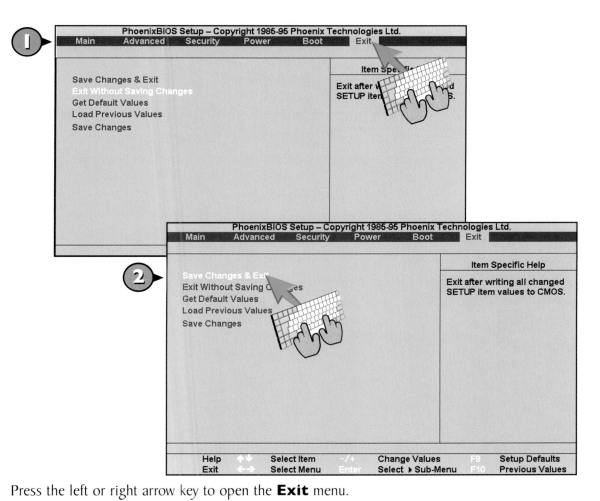

As you change **BIOS** settings, the settings are recorded but not entered. You must save the settings and exit. After you exit, Windows starts.

1 ▶ Press the left or right arrow key to open the **Exit** menu.

2 ▶ Highlight the **Save Changes & Exit** option and press **Enter**.

WARNING
If you change a setting by mistake and are not sure what you did, press the key for returning to the previous settings or values or choose the option for exiting *without* saving changes.

PART 2

Configuring Internet Explorer

By now, you know the basics of Internet Explorer. You can click links to skip from one Web page to another, enter an address to pull up a specific page, use search tools to research topics, and create a list of your favorite sites for quick return trips.

To become a power Web surfer, however, you need to go behind the scenes with Internet Explorer's options and configure Internet Explorer for the way you work. The tasks in this part show you how to use the more advanced Internet Explorer features to customize its layout, start with a different Web page, speed up page loading, and much more.

Tasks

Task 1: Working in Fullscreen Mode

Internet Explorer's toolbars and menus are great when you meet the Web for the first time. However, they just get in the way when you're ready to do some serious Web surfing. To eliminate most of the toolbars and provide more room for displaying Web pages, switch to Fullscreen view.

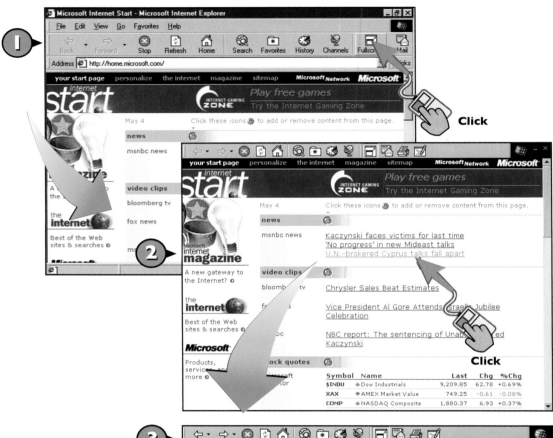

Click

Click

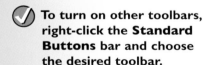 To turn on other toolbars, right-click the **Standard Buttons** bar and choose the desired toolbar.

Click the **Fullscreen** button in Internet Explorer's **Standard Buttons** bar.

Click links to navigate Web pages as you normally would.

You can still use the **Standard Buttons** bar to enter commands, but the rest of the window is hidden.

Click

Click

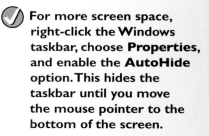

④ ▶ To return to the normal Internet Explorer window, click the **Fullscreen** button again.

⑤ ▶ To exit Internet Explorer in Fullscreen view, click its **Close** button.

✓ **For more screen space, right-click the Windows taskbar, choose Properties, and enable the AutoHide option. This hides the taskbar until you move the mouse pointer to the bottom of the screen.**

End Task

Task 2: Working Offline to Save Time and Money

As you open Web pages, Internet Explorer stores them in a temporary holding area on your hard disk called a cache. If you subscribed to sites to have pages automatically downloaded, they are saved on your disk, too. You can disconnect from the Internet and quickly open these pages from your disk, reducing your connect-time charges.

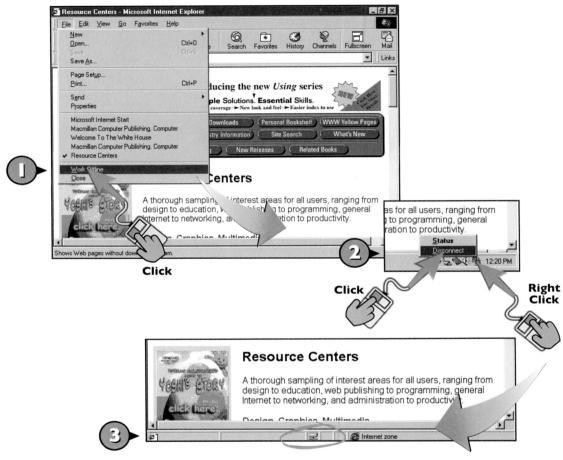

Click

Click

Right
Click

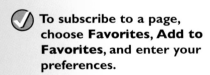
To subscribe to a page, choose **Favorites**, **Add to Favorites**, and enter your preferences.

 Open the **File** menu and choose **Work Offline**.

 Right-click the **Dial-Up Networking** icon in the system tray and choose **Disconnect**.

 An icon appears in Internet Explorer's status bar, indicating that the network connection has been broken.

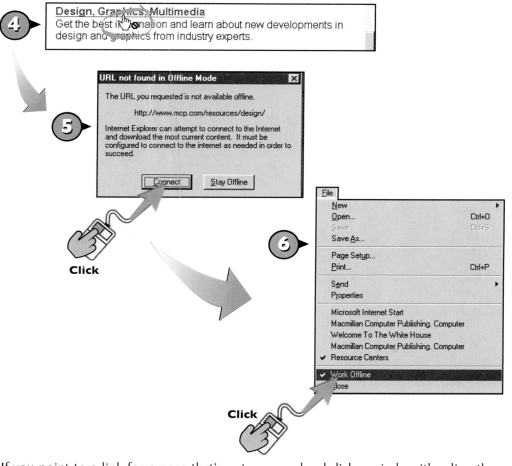

Working offline can save you money, especially if you must dial a long-distance number or are charged for connection time. You can also save time and money by browsing subscribed pages offline.

4 If you point to a link for a page that's not on your hard disk, a circle with a line through it appears next to the pointer.

5 If you click a link for a page that's not on your hard disk, this dialog box appears. Click **Connect**.

6 To go back online, reestablish your Internet connection and then open the **File** menu and choose **Work Offline**.

Task 3: Turning Toolbars On and Off

Although Fullscreen view maximizes the Web page viewing area, it is a little drastic. For a more subtle change, you can turn individual toolbars on or off, including the **Standard Buttons** bar and the **Links** bar.

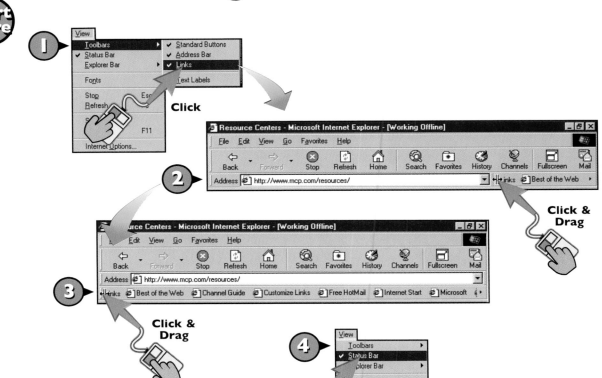

Click

Click & Drag

Click & Drag

Click

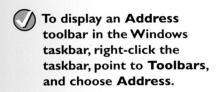

✓ To display an **Address** toolbar in the Windows taskbar, right-click the taskbar, point to **Toolbars**, and choose **Address**.

1 ▶ Open the **View** menu, point to **Toolbars**, and click the name of the toolbar you want to turn on or off.

2 ▶ To resize a toolbar, drag the line on the left end of the toolbar to the left or right.

3 ▶ To move a toolbar, drag the line on the left end of the toolbar up or down and release the mouse button.

4 ▶ To turn the status bar on or off, open the **View** menu and choose **Status Bar**.

End Task

Task 4: Picking a Different Font Size

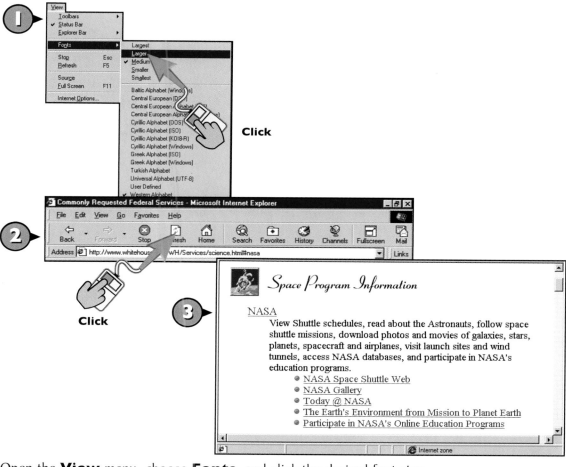

Click

Click

Every Web page has codes (tags) that work behind the scenes to tell the Web browser how to display text. If the text is too large or too small, you can change the way that Internet Explorer interprets the tags to control the text size and style.

✓ For additional font control, choose **View, Internet Options** and then click the Fonts button.

① Open the **View** menu, choose **Fonts**, and click the desired font size.

② If the new font size does not change the appearance of text on the current page, click the **Refresh** button.

③ The page appears with larger or smaller text.

ⓘ **WARNING**
Some pages have more specific font codes that override the font settings in Internet Explorer.

Task 5: Accessing the Internet Options

To change most of the settings that control the appearance and performance of Internet Explorer, you must first display the **Internet Options** dialog box. Here, you learn how to access the Internet Options. Later tasks show you how to change specific settings.

Start Here

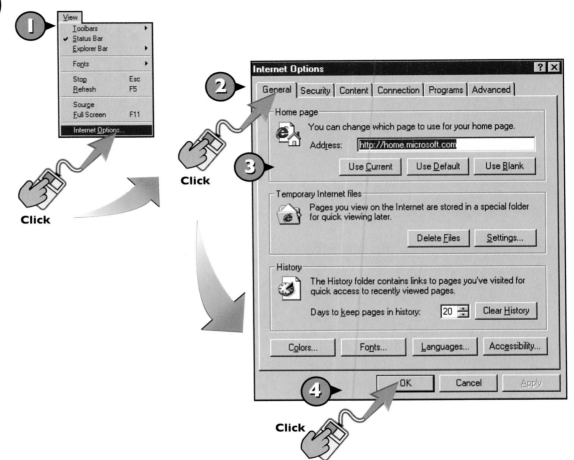

Click

Click

Click

1 ▶ Open the **View** menu and choose **Internet Options**.

2 ▶ Click a tab for the settings you want to change.

3 ▶ Enter your preferences.

4 ▶ Click the **OK** button to close the dialog box and save your changes.

End Task

Task 6: Starting with a Different Home Page

Start Here

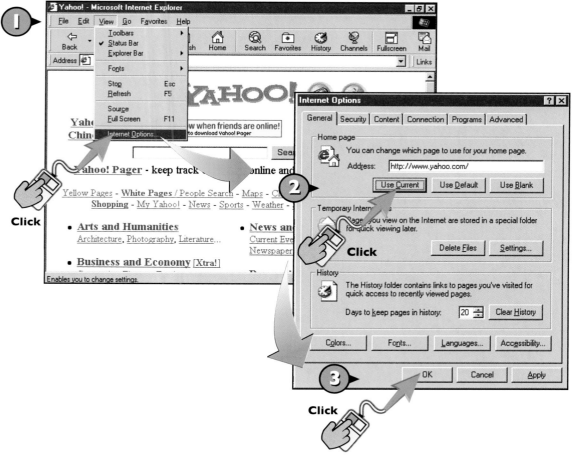

Click

Click

Click

Whenever you start Internet Explorer, it automatically loads a page, called the *home page*. Unless you change it, you will be greeted by Microsoft's home page every time you start Internet Explorer. To start with a different page, enter its address in the **Internet Options** dialog box.

Display the page you want to use as your home page and then choose **View**, **Internet Options**.

Click the **Use Current** button to insert the page's address in the **Address** text box.

Click **OK**.

✓ If you usually connect to the Internet to search for information, use your favorite search page as your home page.

✓ You can type a Web page address in the **Address** text box instead of clicking the **Use Current** button. Be sure to precede the address with **http://**.

End Task

Task 7: Entering Preferences for Temporary Internet Files

Internet Explorer uses a percentage of your hard disk to store Web pages and associated files, such as graphics. When you return to a page you've recently visited, Internet Explorer loads the page from your hard disk, so it opens faster. You can specify the amount of disk space Internet Explorer should use.

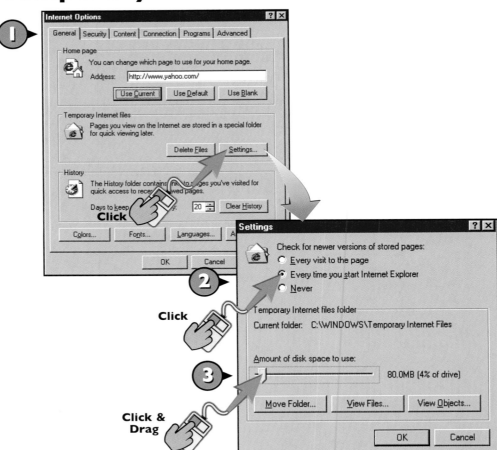

✓ If you're low on disk space, decrease the amount of disk space that Internet Explorer uses. For better browser performance, increase the amount.

1 ▶ On the **General** tab of the **Internet Options** dialog box, click the **Settings** button.

2 ▶ Choose the desired option to specify how often you want Internet Explorer to check for page updates.

3 ▶ Drag the **Amount of disk space to use** slider to specify the percentage of your hard disk to use for temporary files.

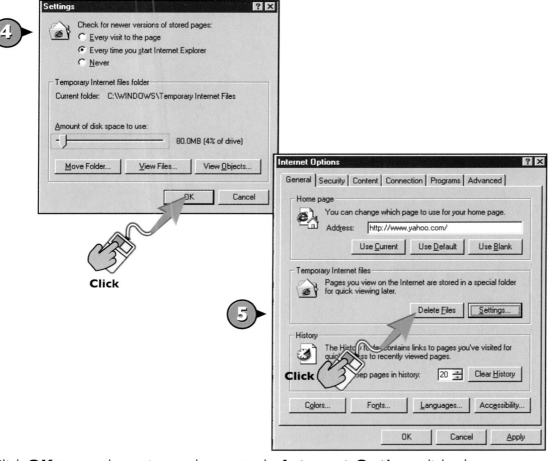

If you're in immediate need of extra disk space, you can have Internet Explorer delete all temporary Internet files.

Click

Click

4 ▶ Click **OK** to save the settings and return to the **Internet Options** dialog box.

5 ▶ To delete any temporary Internet files, click the **Delete Files** button.

✓ **Use Disk Cleanup regularly to clear temporary files from your hard disk. See Part 1, Task 2, "Reclaiming Disk Space with Disk Cleanup."**

✓ **Windows checks the Web for updates to cached pages every time you start Internet Explorer. To make sure you have the latest Web pages, choose Every visit to the page. To speed up browsing, choose Never.**

Task 8: Changing the History Settings

Internet Explorer records the address of every Web page you visit and stores the addresses on a *history list*. You can click the **History** button to display the list, which contains links for Web pages you've visited during the last couple weeks. To have Internet Explorer keep track of pages for a longer or shorter time period, adjust the settings as desired.

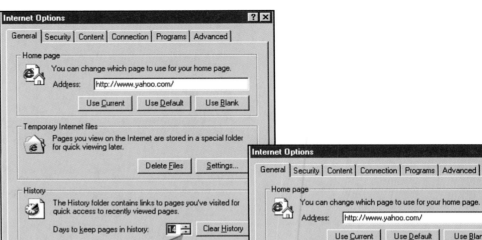

Click

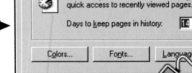

Click

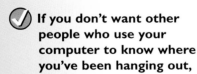

 If you don't want other people who use your computer to know where you've been hanging out, clear the history list.

 In the **General** tab of the **Internet Options** dialog box, click the up or down arrow next to the **Days to keep pages in history** box to set the desired number of days.

To erase the history list, click the **Clear History** button.

Task 9: Changing the Default Web Page Colors

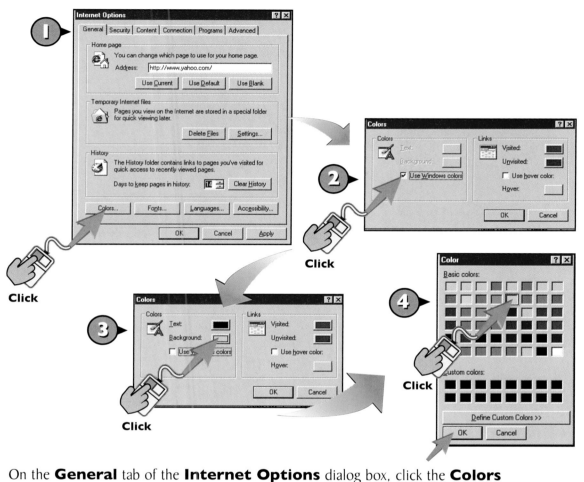

Click

Click

Click

2

3

4

Click

Click

Because Web pages use codes to specify formatting, such as text and background colors, you can control the appearance of most Web pages by setting your preferences in Internet Explorer.

① On the **General** tab of the **Internet Options** dialog box, click the **Colors** button.

② To specify your color preferences, click **Use Windows colors** to remove the check mark.

③ Click the **Text** or **Background** button.

④ Choose the desired color for the Web page text or background and click **OK**.

WARNING
Many Web pages use background colors or graphics that override the settings in Internet Explorer.

You can also change the colors Internet Explorer uses for links.

Task 10: Entering Security Zone Settings

Internet Explorer warns you before submitting sensitive information on a form or downloading a program that could possibly contain a virus. To tighten or relax these warnings, you can use *security zones*. There are four zones: Local (intranet), Trusted (for sites you trust), Restricted (for sites you don't trust), and Internet (for all other sites).

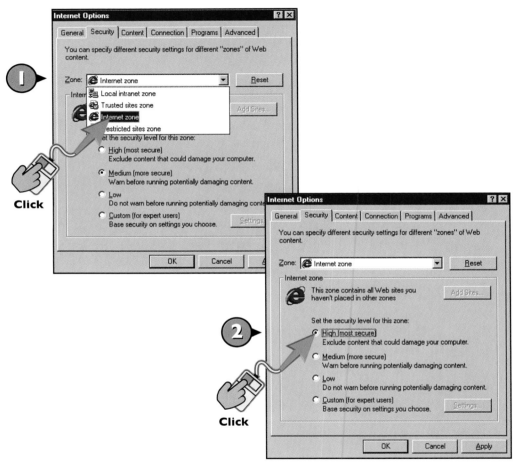

✓ If you relax security, you can safely submit information on a form if you see a padlock icon in the status bar.

1 In the **Security** tab of the **Internet Options** dialog box, open the **Zone** drop-down list and choose the zone whose settings you want to change.

2 Click the desired security setting for this zone: **High**, **Medium**, or **Low**.

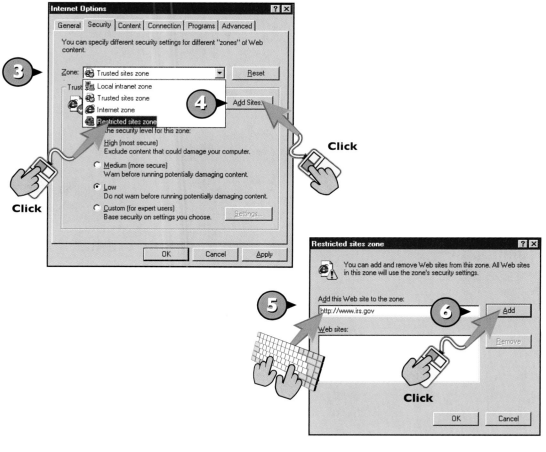

To prevent security messages from popping up at sites you completely trust, you can add the sites to the Trusted zone. To protect yourself on sites you don't trust, you can add the sites to the Restricted zone.

③ To add a Web site to a zone, open the **Zone** drop-down list and click the desired zone.

④ Click the **Add Sites** button.

⑤ Type the address of the site you want to add to the zone. (Be sure to type **http://** at the start of the address.)

⑥ Click the **Add** button. (Click **OK** when you are done adding sites to the zone.)

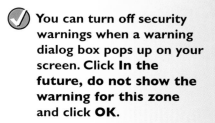

You can turn off security warnings when a warning dialog box pops up on your screen. Click In the future, do not show the warning for this zone and click OK.

Task 11: Entering Additional Security Settings

Although the security zones address most of the Web security issues, they don't warn you before a Web site sends you a cookie or if data you submit on a form is redirected to another site. Although the risks are slight, you may want to enter security settings tighten security for these events.

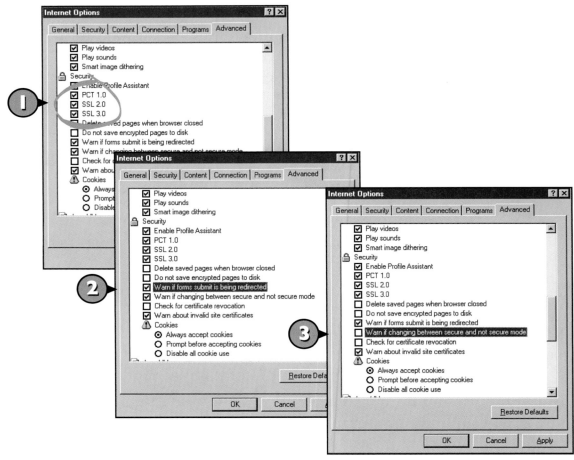

✓ **PCT (Private Communication Technology) and SSL (Secure Sockets Layer) are security standards that Internet Explorer and many Web page forms support. When you are at a site that supports these standards, Internet Explorer displays a padlock icon in the status bar.**

 In the **Advanced** tab of the **Internet Options** dialog box, scroll down to **Security** and make sure **PCT 1.0**, **SSL 2.0**, and **SSL 3.0** are all checked.

 To ensure that data on your form is not sent to a different site, turn on **Warn if forms submit is being redirected**.

 You can safely turn off **Warn if changing between secure and not secure mode**.

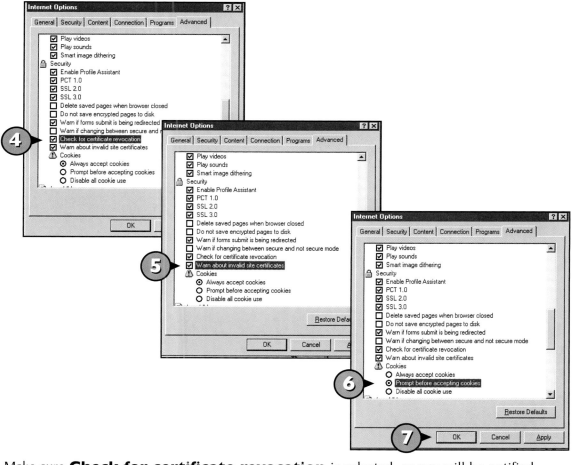

Internet security is similar to airport security. Whenever you consider tightening security, ask yourself if the added safety is worth the inconvenience. You don't want error messages popping up on your screen every time you click a link.

4 ▶ Make sure **Check for certificate revocation** is selected, so you will be notified when a site loses its security certificate.

5 ▶ Make sure **Warn about invalid site certificates** is checked.

6 ▶ Under **Cookies**, choose the desired option to accept cookies, reject them, or be prompted before accepting.

7 ▶ When you are satisfied with your selections, click **OK**.

Cookies are bits of computer code that can record your browsing habits and keep track of items you order. Most cookies are intended to enhance your experience on the Web.

End Task

Task 12: Censoring Web Page Content

The Web contains its fair share of offensive material, including pages with violence, sex, foul language, and racist comments. Fortunately, Internet Explorer's Content Advisor can block access to most sites that contain offensive content.

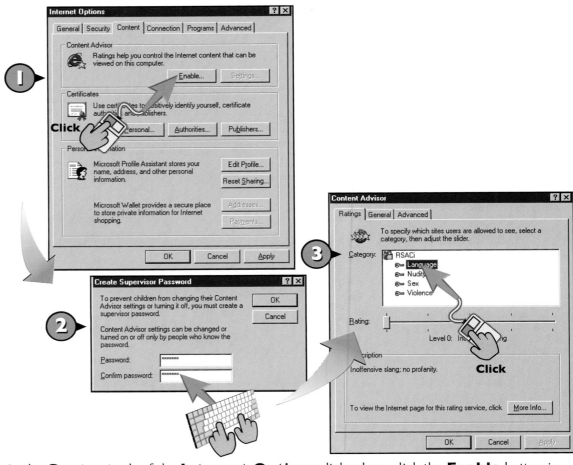

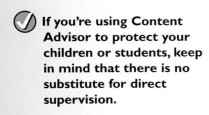 If you're using Content Advisor to protect your children or students, keep in mind that there is no substitute for direct supervision.

In the **Content** tab of the **Internet Options** dialog box, click the **Enable** button in the **Content Advisor** section.

Type your password in the **Password** and **Confirm password** text boxes, and click **OK**.

In the **Content Advisor** dialog box, click a category to tighten or relax censoring for that category.

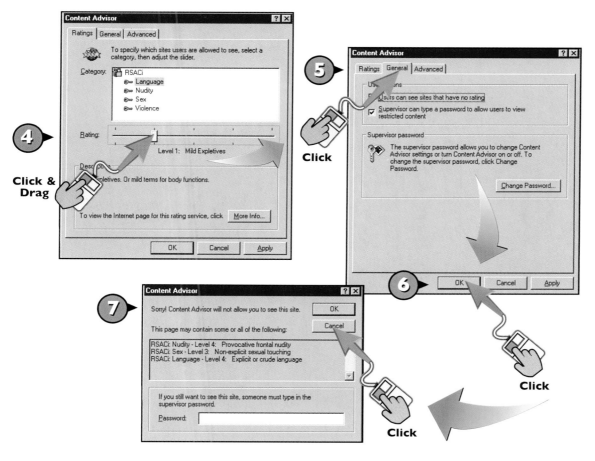

Web censoring programs are not perfect. Most use a rating system that relies on the Web site administrators to rate their pages. If you choose to block access to unrated sites, you'll be banned from most Web sites, even the clean ones.

Click & Drag

Click

Click

Click

✅ Turn on **Users can see sites that have no rating**, or you won't be able to access many sites.

✅ To change any Content Advisor settings later, including your password, display the **Internet Options** dialog box, click the **Content** tab, and click the **Settings** button.

4 ▶ Drag the slider to the right to allow access to a wider range of sites or to the left to tighten restrictions.

5 ▶ Click the **General** tab and enter your preferences for accessing unrated sites and prompting for a password at restricted sites.

6 ▶ Click **OK**, and then close the **Internet Options** dialog box.

7 ▶ When you try to access a censored site, Content Advisor prohibits it. Click **Cancel** to go elsewhere.

End Task

Internet Explorer can automatically launch Dial-Up Networking and connect to the Internet for you. This is useful if you subscribe to Web sites or you just don't want to deal with the **Connect To** dialog box every time you run Internet Explorer.

Task 13: Dialing In to the Internet Automatically

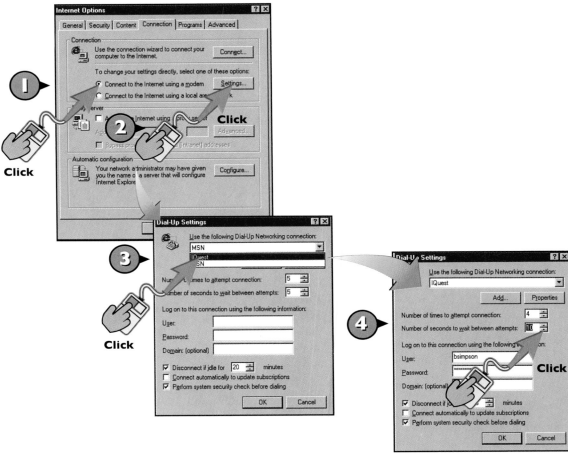

✓ **AutoConnect works for Outlook Express, too, so you can schedule Outlook Express to automatically check for and retrieve email messages.**

 In the **Connection** tab of the **Internet Options** dialog box, click the desired option for connecting via modem or network.

 If you connect to the Internet using a modem, click the **Settings** button (this option is unavailable for network connections).

 If you have more than one Dial-Up Networking connection, choose the connection you want to use.

4 Set the number of times you want Internet Explorer to attempt the connection and the number of seconds to wait between attempts.

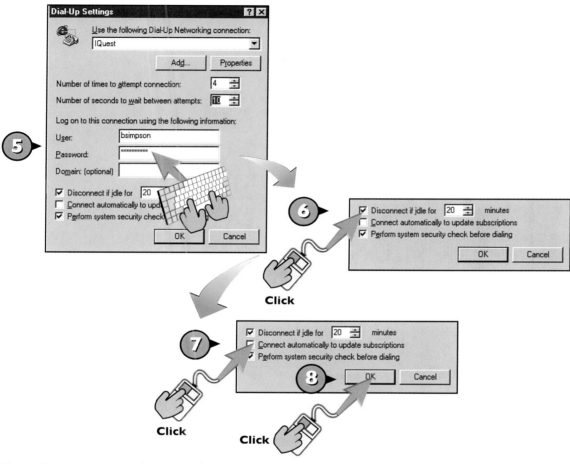

If you set up site subscriptions and you leave your computer on, Internet Explorer will run automatically at the scheduled time, download the subscribed pages, and disconnect. You can then view the pages offline, as shown in Task 2, "Working Offline to Save Time and Money."

Click

Click   **Click**

 Enter the username and password you use to connect to your service provider.

 Place a check in the **Disconnect if idle for** box and set the number of minutes Internet Explorer should wait before disconnecting.

 Place a check in the **Connect automatically to update subscriptions** box.

 Click **OK**.

 WARNING
If you're concerned that Internet Explorer is going to rack up a huge Internet or phone bill downloading subscribed pages, turn off **Connect automatically to update subscriptions.**

Task 14: Running Outlook Express from Internet Explorer

Internet Explorer is more than just a Web browser. It is a suite of Internet programs, including Outlook Express for email and newsgroups. To run Outlook Express from Internet Explorer using the **Mail** button, you must set up Internet Explorer to use it.

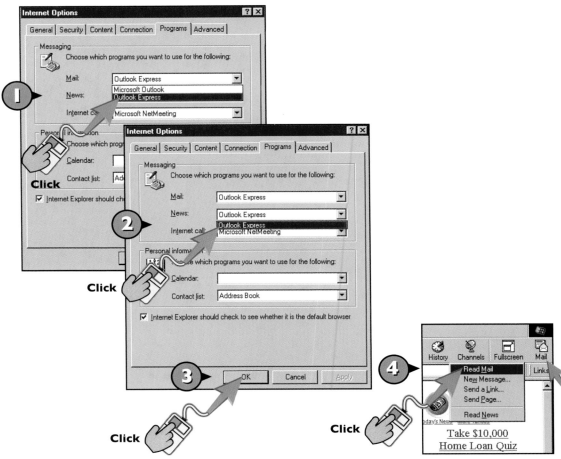

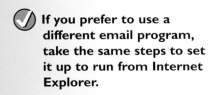

✓ If you prefer to use a different email program, take the same steps to set it up to run from Internet Explorer.

1 In the **Programs** tab of the **Internet Options** dialog box, open the **Mail** drop-down list and choose **Outlook Express**.

2 Open the **News** drop-down list and choose **Outlook Express**.

3 Click **OK**.

4 To run Outlook Express from Internet Explorer, click the **Mail** button and choose **Read Mail** or **New Message**.

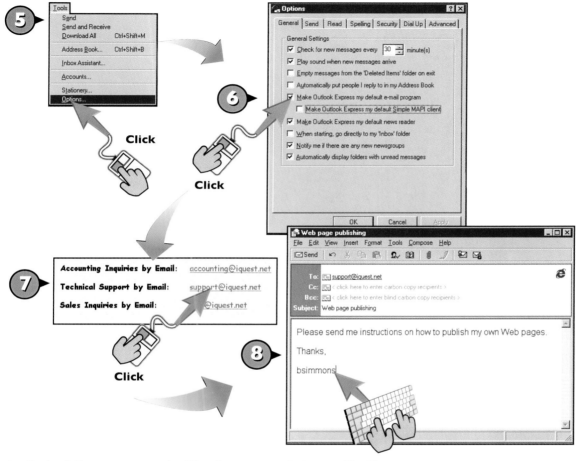

Some Web pages contain links that point to newsgroups or email addresses. For instance, you might encounter a page that contains a link for contacting the creator of the page. You can have Outlook Express run automatically when you click the link and address a new message to the person.

5 In Outlook Express, open the **Tools** menu and choose **Options**.

6 Turn on the options for using Outlook Express as your default email program and news reader. Click **OK**.

7 In Internet Explorer, click a Web page link for contacting a person via email.

8 Outlook Express automatically starts and addresses a new message to the person. Compose and send the message.

 See Part 4, "Configuring Outlook Express," for more instructions on customizing Outlook Express.

Task 15: Entering Browsing Settings

Internet Explorer offers several settings that control the way Internet Explorer behaves as you browse the Web, including using AutoComplete for addresses you type and starting Internet Explorer in Fullscreen mode.

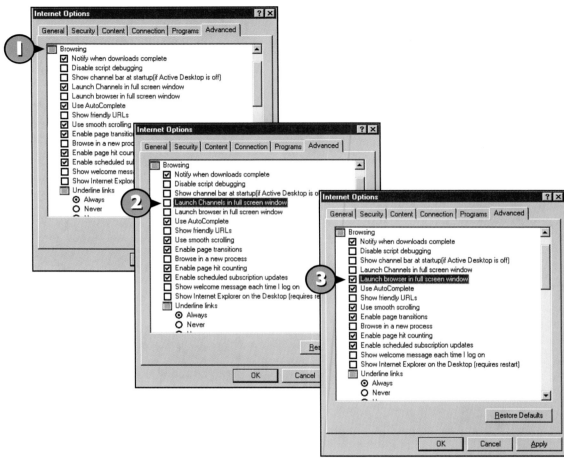

✔ Clicking the **Channels** button in Internet Explorer lets the **Channel bar** take over your screen. To have it appear as a bar in the Internet Explorer window, turn off **Launch Channels in full screen window**.

1 In the **Advanced** tab of the **Internet Options** dialog box, scroll down to the **Browsing** options.

2 To have Internet Explorer display channels in a normal window, turn off **Launch Channels in full screen window**.

3 To have Internet Explorer start in Fullscreen mode, turn on **Launch browser in full screen window**.

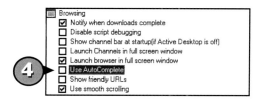

These few steps cover the main **Browsing** options but do not cover all the available options. For information about a **Browsing** option that's not covered here, right-click the option and choose **What's This?**

4 ▶ If you don't like the AutoComplete feature, you can click it to turn it off.

5 ▶ Turn on **Show friendly URLs** to have Internet Explorer's status bar display a page name rather than complete address when you point to a link.

6 ▶ To prevent Internet Explorer from automatically dialing out, turn off **Enable scheduled subscription updates**.

7 ▶ Choose the desired option for displaying underlined links.

✓ With AutoComplete, you type the first few characters of a Web page address (for a page you already visited), and Internet Explorer inserts the rest of the address for you.

✓ If you have trouble scrolling Web pages, turn off **Use smooth scrolling**.

Task 16: Loading Pages Faster Without Graphics

Graphics, audio and video clips, and other media are what really breathe life into the Web. However, these media files are typically large and can take a long time to download over a modem connection. To reduce the time it takes to download pages, you can have Internet Explorer omit the fancy stuff.

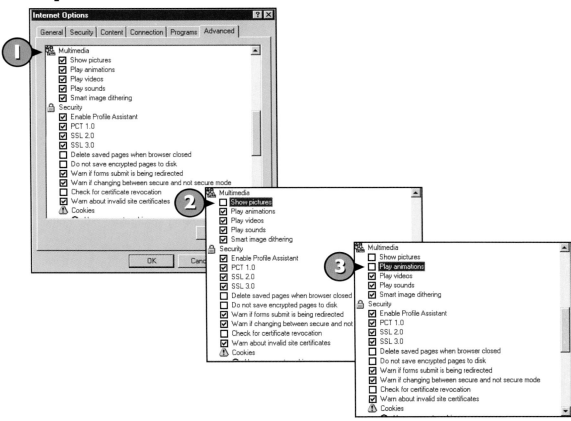

 If you disable the **Show pictures** option, Internet Explorer displays icons in place of the pictures. To see a picture, right-click the icon and choose **Show Picture**.

1 In the **Advanced** tab of the **Internet Options** dialog box, scroll down to the **Multimedia** options.

2 Turn off **Show pictures** to have Internet Explorer omit any graphics that the page may have.

3 Turn off **Play animations** to prevent animated graphics from playing.

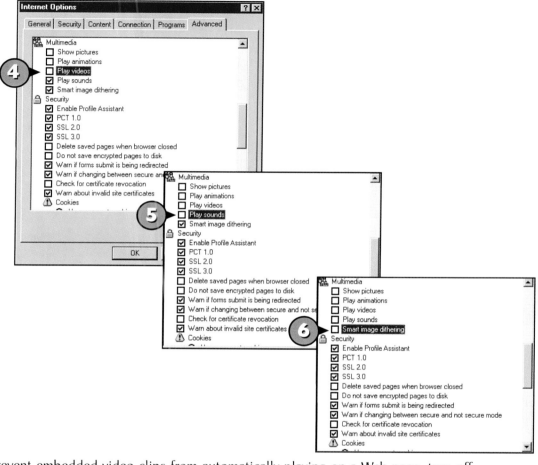

Video clips are notorious for slowing down Web page loading, because they are typically very large. Fortunately, most Web pages don't play video clips automatically.

4 To prevent embedded video clips from automatically playing on a Web page, turn off **Play videos**.

5 To prevent pages from automatically playing audio clips, turn off **Play sounds**.

6 To prevent Internet Explorer from smoothing out rough graphics, you can turn off **Smart image dithering**.

✓ If a Web page plays a video clip right on the page, the clip is said to be embedded. You can still play clips that are not embedded by clicking the clip's link.

✓ Audio clips are typically small, at least compared to large graphic files and video clips.

Task 17: Downloading and Installing ActiveX Controls

Although Internet Explorer can open Web pages and play a wide range of media files, you will encounter media files that Internet Explorer cannot play. To play these files, you must download and install the required ActiveX control.

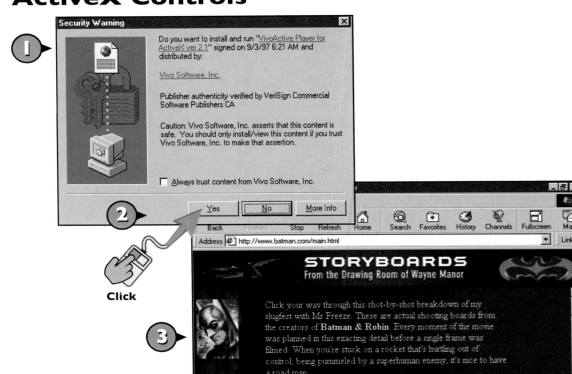

Start Here

Click

✓ Choose **Help, Product Updates** to download and install Microsoft Internet components for Internet Explorer.

✓ If the ActiveX control has not been certified, cancel the download.

1 When you connect to a Web page that has ActiveX content, Internet Explorer prompts you to download the required control.

2 Make sure the control has been certified before giving your okay, and then click **Yes**.

3 The ActiveX component plays right on the Web page.

Next Step

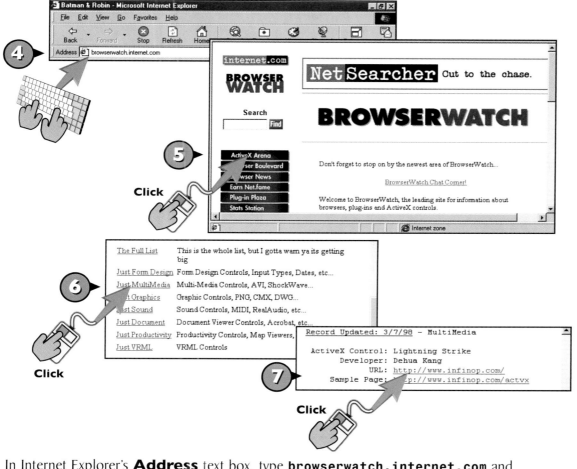

Although most Web sites will prompt you to download the required **ActiveX** control, some will not. In such cases, you must find the required **ActiveX** control on the Web. You can find links to popular **ActiveX** controls at the following sites:

`browserwatch.internet.com`

`cws.internet.com`

`www.tucows.com`

4 In Internet Explorer's **Address** text box, type `browserwatch.internet.com` and press **Enter**.

5 Click the link for ActiveX controls.

6 Click the link for the desired category of controls.

7 Click the link for connecting to the Web site where you'll find the control, and follow the instructions at that site.

Task 18: Editing File Associations

When you install an **ActiveX** control (or almost any Windows program), Windows creates a file association that links the program to a file type. You click the file's icon or link, and Windows automatically starts the associated program and plays the file. If you would rather use a different program to play the file, you can edit the file association.

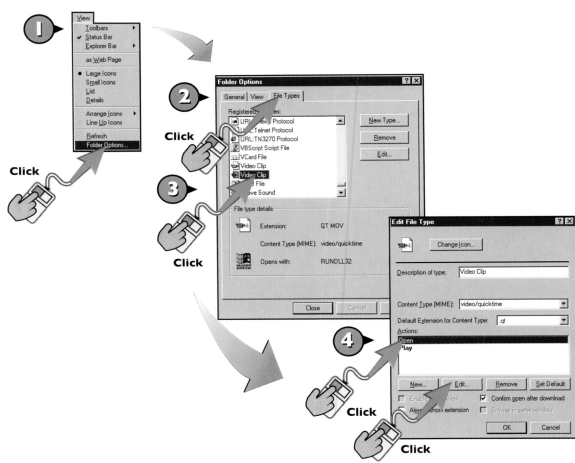

Start Here

Click

Click

Click

Click

Click

Click

① In My Computer or Windows Explorer, open the **View** menu and select **Folder Options**.

② Click the **File Types** tab and scroll down the list of registered file types.

③ Highlight the file type you want to associate with a different program and then click the **Edit** button.

④ In the **Actions** section of the **Edit File Type** dialog box, click **Open** and then click the **Edit** button.

Next Step

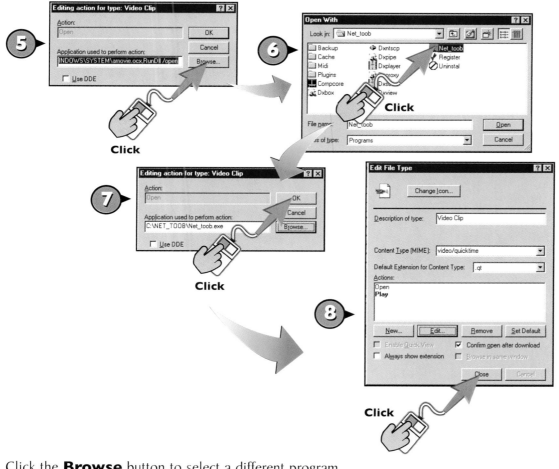

If you click a link for a file that is not associated to a program, Windows displays a dialog box prompting you to open the file or save it to disk. If you choose to open the file, Windows displays a list of programs installed on your computer. Choose a program that is capable of opening the selected file type.

5 ▶ Click the **Browse** button to select a different program.

6 ▶ Change to the desired program's disk and folder, select the file that starts the program, and click **Open**.

7 ▶ Click **OK**.

8 ▶ Click **Close** to return to the **Folder Options** dialog box, and then click **OK** to save your changes.

 Sometimes it is easier to delete the current file association for a particular file type and then create a new association from scratch.

Mastering the New Active Desktop

The biggest improvement introduced in Windows 98 is the *Active Desktop*, an interface that integrates the Windows desktop with the Web. With the Active Desktop, you can navigate your local PC, network, and company intranet just as easily as you can navigate remotely stored Web pages—by single-clicking *links* rather than double-clicking icons.

In addition, the Active Desktop serves as an information center. You can place live components (from the Web) right on your Windows desktop to display up-to-the-minute news, weather, sports, and other information. The tasks in this part show you how to turn on the Active Desktop, reorient yourself in Windows, and customize your desktop for the way you work (and play).

Tasks

Task 1: Turning On Web Style

Start Here

You are probably accustomed to double-clicking icons to display the contents of a disk, open a folder, and run programs. Windows 98 makes these actions easier by giving you single-click access to disks, folders, and files, just as if you were clicking links on a Web page. To take advantage of single-click access, you must turn on Web style.

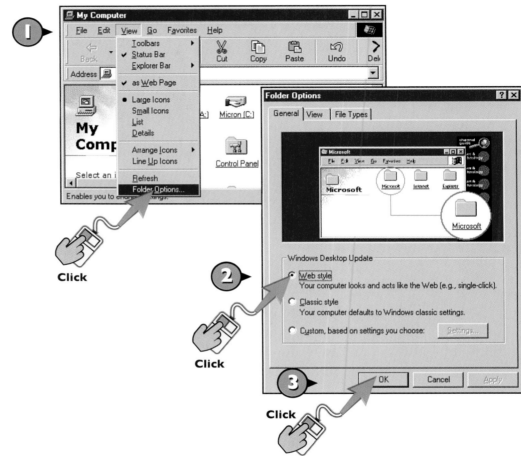

Click

Click

Click

✓ For more control of your desktop, click **Custom**, click the **Settings** button, and enter your preferences.

1 ▶ In My Computer, open the **View** menu and choose **Folder Options**.

2 ▶ Click **Web style**.

3 ▶ Click **OK**.

End Task

Task 2: Opening Files and Running Applications in Web Style

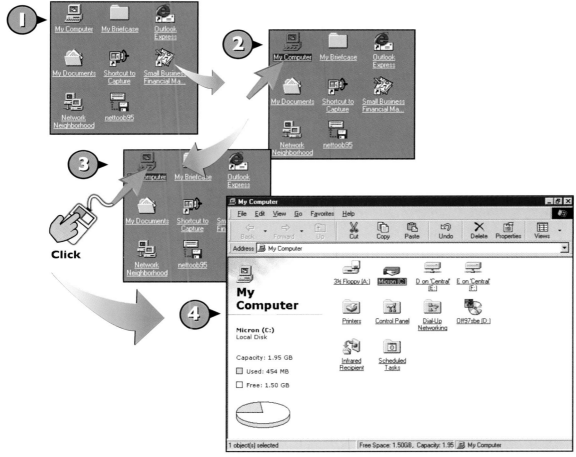

Click

Although Web style offers quicker access to your computer's resources, it takes some getting used to. You'll be tempted to click when you need to point and double-click when a single click will do. With these steps and a little practice, you'll have no trouble making the transition.

1 With Web style on, shortcut and icon names appear underlined.

2 Rest the mouse pointer on an icon to select (highlight) it.

3 Click an icon to activate it.

4 In Web style, the left side of the **My Computer** window displays useful information about the highlighted object.

✓ If you don't like single-click access, repeat the steps in the previous task and choose **Classic style**.

⚠ **WARNING**
If you highlight more than one document file and then click one of the selected files, Windows will open all the documents.

Task 3: Selecting Files and Folders in Web Style

In order to copy, move, or delete files or folders, you must first select them. When you need to select, just remember to point to (rest the mouse pointer on) the object, instead of clicking it. You can also use the **Ctrl** and **Shift** keys while pointing to select multiple files or folders.

Ctrl+**Click**

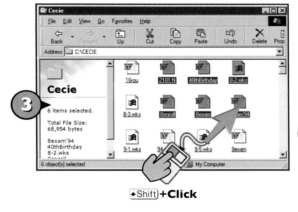

◆Shift+**Click**

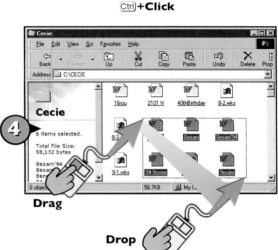

Drag

Drop

✓ Web style makes it a little tougher to rename files and folders. You can't click once, click again, and then type a new name, as you could in Windows 95. Instead, select the file or folder, press **F2**, and rename it.

1 ▶ Point to a file or folder to select it.

2 ▶ To select multiple, non-neighboring files or folders, **Ctrl+point** to their icons.

3 ▶ To select neighboring objects, point to the first object and then **Shift+point** to the last object in the group.

4 ▶ You can also drag a selection box around neighboring files, but don't click an icon when you hold down the mouse button to drag.

End Task

Task 4: Browsing the Web with Windows Explorer

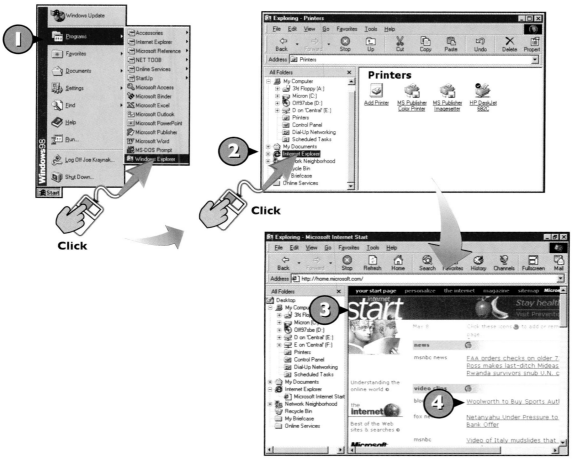

Click

Click

In Windows 98, Windows Explorer and Internet Explorer have joined forces. In addition to giving you single-click access to your disks, folders, and files, these programs work together to allow you to open Web pages right from Windows Explorer.

 Connect to the Internet and then choose **Start**, **Programs**, **Windows Explorer**.

 In Windows Explorer, scroll down the folder list and click **Internet Explorer**.

 Windows Explorer loads the home page that Internet Explorer is set up to open on startup.

 You can click buttons, enter Web page addresses, and click links to navigate the Web.

To quickly run Windows Explorer, right-click the **Start** button or a disk or folder icon and choose **Explore.**

Task 5: Customizing Your Folders

Web style and Classic style give you an either/or choice between the way My Computer works in Windows 98 and the way it worked in Windows 95. However, you can enter your own preferences to make My Computer look and act the way *you* want it to.

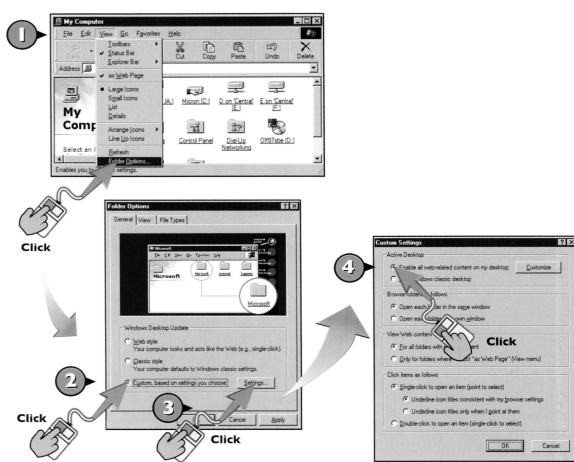

Click

Click

Click

Click

✓ To use a graphic or Web page as a background for a folder, open the folder, choose **View, Customize This Folder**, and enter your preferences.

> **I** In My Computer, open the **View** menu and choose **Folder Options**.

> **2** Click **Custom, based on settings you choose**.

> **3** Click the **Settings** button.

> **4** Under **Active Desktop**, choose the desired option for viewing the desktop in Web or Classic style.

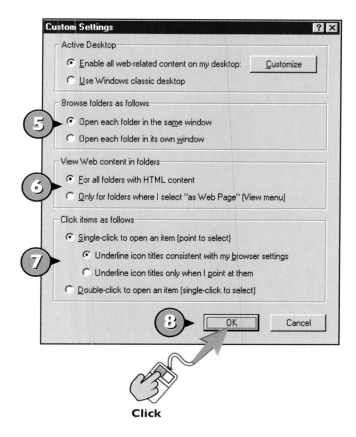

Click

5 Under **Browse folders as follows**, you can choose to have folders you click open in the same window or in a separate window.

6 To turn off the information bar on the left side of the **My Computer** window, choose **Only for folders where I select "as Web Page"**.

7 Under **Click items as follows**, choose the desired option for single-click or double-click file access.

8 Click **OK**.

✓ To make all folders look the same, open the folder you want them to look like. Choose **View, Folder Options,** click the **View** tab, and click **Like Current Folder.** You can enter additional configuration settings on this tab.

✓ To turn the information bar on the left side of the **My Computer** window on or off for individual folders, open the **View** menu and choose **as Web Page.**

End Task

Task 6: Displaying the Windows Desktop as a Web Page

Your choice of Classic or Web style in My Computer controls the way the Windows shortcut icons appear and behave on the Windows desktop. However, the desktop has additional features, such as Web page backgrounds and Active Desktop components, that you can use only if you choose to view the desktop as a Web page.

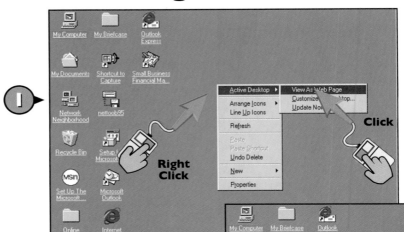

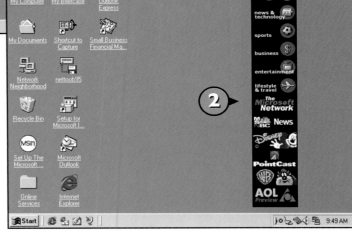

 If you chose Web style in My Computer, the names of the shortcuts on the desktop appear underlined regardless of whether **View As Web Page** is on or off.

1 Right-click a blank area of the Windows desktop and choose **Active Desktop**, **View As Web Page**.

2 The **Channel** bar appears on the desktop. See Task 15, "Tuning In to the Web with the Channel Bar," for details.

Task 7: Touring the Windows Active Desktop

Start Here

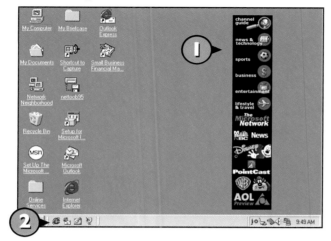

Although the Active Desktop doesn't look much different from the Windows 95 desktop, it offers several enhancements, including single-click icons, the Channel bar, a new Quick Launch toolbar for running programs, and drag-and-drop support for the Start menu.

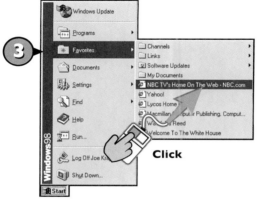

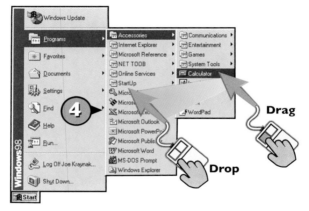

Drag

Click

Drop

 The **Channel** bar is an Active Desktop component. You can add components from the Web to the desktop.

 The **Quick Launch** toolbar gives you single-click access to Internet Explorer, Outlook Express, the desktop, and channels.

 The **Start** menu includes a **Favorites** submenu that allows you to quickly open Web pages you have marked as your favorites.

 To move a program or submenu on the **Start** menu (or one of its submenus), drag it to the desired location.

 To see how to download and install additional Active Desktop components, see Task 14, "Adding Active Desktop Components from the Web."

 To learn how to use and configure the **Quick Launch** toolbar and use additional toolbars, see Tasks 9–13 in this part.

 End Task

Task 8: Using a Web Page as the Windows Background

The new desktop consists of two layers: an *HTML layer* and an *icon layer*. HTML (short for Hypertext Markup Language) is a system of codes used to format Web pages. By using HTML to control your desktop, Internet Explorer transforms your desktop into a Web page. You can even use a Web page as the desktop background.

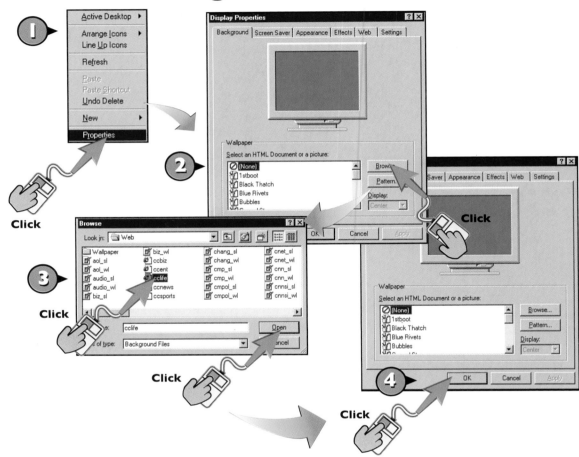

(✓) You can use FrontPage Express (Start, Programs, Internet Explorer, FrontPage Express) to design your own Web page to use as a background.

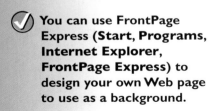

1 Right-click a blank area of the desktop and choose **Properties**.

2 Under **Wallpaper**, click **Browse**.

3 Navigate to the **Windows\Web** or **Windows\Web\Wallpaper** folder. Click the desired wallpaper design and click **Open**.

4 Click **OK** to close the **Display Properties** dialog box.

End Task

Task 9: Running Applications from the Quick Launch Toolbar

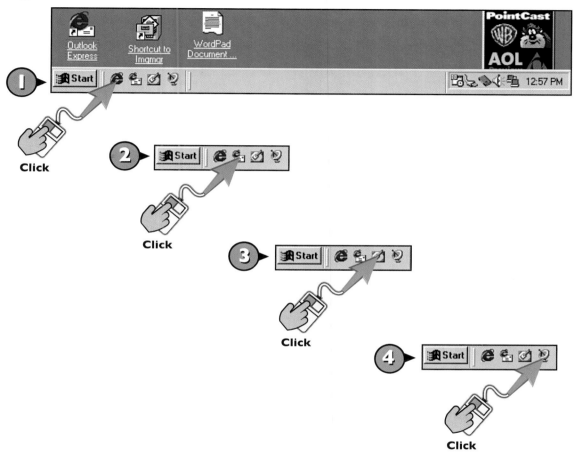

Click

Click

Click

Click

The **Quick Launch** toolbar gives you single-click access to programs without cluttering your desktop with additional shortcuts. In addition, the **Show Desktop** button provides a direct flight to the desktop by minimizing all open program windows. Here, you learn how to save time with this new toolbar.

1 To run Internet Explorer, click the **Launch Internet Explorer Browser** button.

2 To run Outlook Express, click the **Launch Outlook Express** button.

3 To minimize all open windows and return to the Windows desktop, click the **Show Desktop** button.

4 To display Web channels, click the **View Channels** button.

To reduce desktop clutter, delete the desktop shortcuts for Internet Explorer and Outlook Express and run these programs from the **Quick Launch** toolbar.

End Task

Task 10: Adding Shortcuts to the Quick Launch Toolbar

After realizing the power of the **Quick Launch** toolbar, you may want to use it to run other programs. You can add all sorts of objects to the **Quick Launch** toolbar, including program icons, disk and folder icons, document icons, and shortcuts.

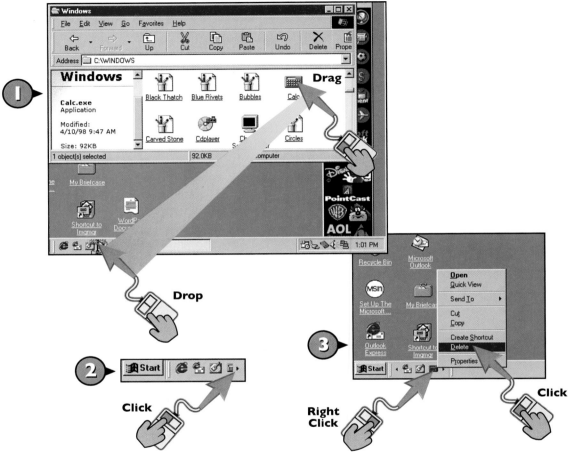

✓ Right-drag a program from the **Start, Programs** menu over the **Quick Launch** toolbar, release the mouse button, and choose **Create Shortcut(s) Here** to place a button for it on the **Quick Launch** toolbar.

1 ► In My Computer, display the disk, folder, file, or program icon you want to add to the **Quick Launch** toolbar. Drag the icon to the desired position, and release the mouse button.

2 ► If the **Quick Launch** toolbar has more buttons than it can display, click the arrow to scroll them into view.

3 ► To remove a button from the **Quick Launch** toolbar, right-click the button and choose **Delete**.

Task 11: Resizing and Moving the Quick Launch Toolbar

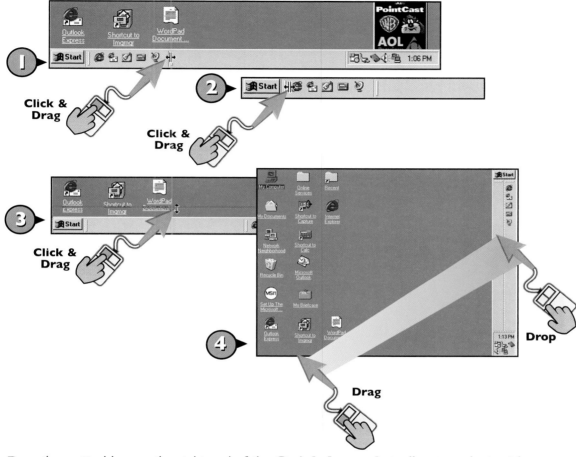

The **Quick Launch** toolbar is large enough to hold only a few buttons. To make more room, you can resize it. You can also move it to a more convenient location.

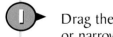 Drag the vertical bar on the right end of the **Quick Launch** toolbar to make it wider or narrower.

 Drag the vertical bar on the left end of the **Quick Launch** toolbar to the right to move it.

 To give yourself additional room for buttons and toolbars, drag the top of the taskbar up.

 To move the taskbar, drag a blank area of the taskbar to another edge of the desktop.

 If the taskbar takes up too much space, right-click it, choose **Properties**, and turn on **AutoHide**. This tucks the taskbar out of the way. To bring it back into view, move the mouse pointer to the edge of the screen where the taskbar is hidden.

Task 12: Turning on Additional Taskbar Toolbars

The **Quick Launch** toolbar is a great tool, but it contains buttons for items you can already access from the desktop. Fortunately, Microsoft built in some additional toolbars, including the **Address** toolbar, which contains a text box that you can use to enter Web page addresses. These steps show you how to turn on these additional toolbars.

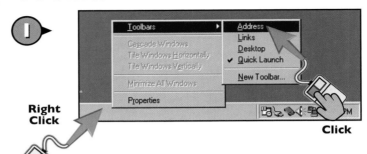

Right Click

Click

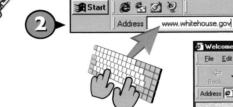

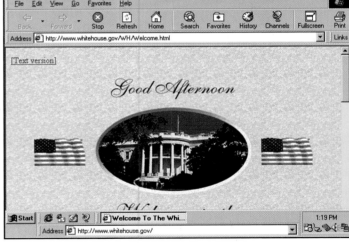

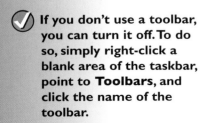 If you don't use a toolbar, you can turn it off. To do so, simply right-click a blank area of the taskbar, point to **Toolbars**, and click the name of the toolbar.

 Right-click a blank area of the taskbar, point to **Toolbars**, and click the name of the toolbar you want to turn on.

 The selected toolbar is inserted in the taskbar. With the **Address** toolbar, type a Web page address and press **Enter**.

 Internet Explorer runs and opens the Web page.

Task 13: Transforming a Folder into a Taskbar Toolbar

Start Here

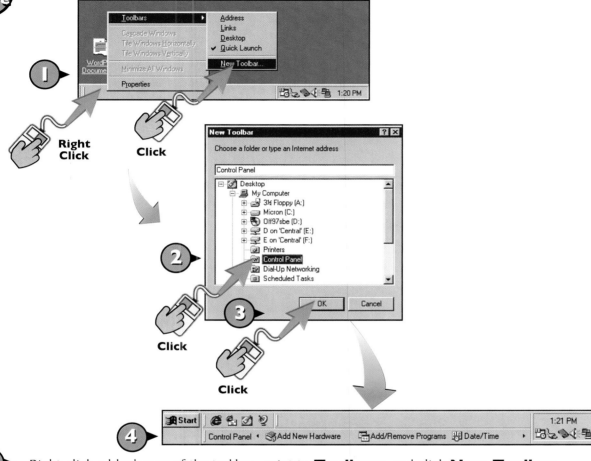

Right Click

Click

Click

Click

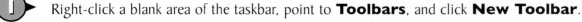

In addition to the ready-made taskbar toolbars that Windows offers, you can create a toolbar that displays the contents of any disk or folder, including My Computer, the Control Panel, and the Printers folder. These steps show you how to do it.

1. Right-click a blank area of the taskbar, point to **Toolbars**, and click **New Toolbar**.

2. Navigate to the folder whose contents you want to add as a new taskbar toolbar.

3. Click **OK**.

4. Windows creates a toolbar for the folder and displays each icon in the folder as a button on the toolbar.

✓ When you create a new toolbar out of a folder, the folder's name is added to the **Toolbars** submenu, so you can easily turn it off.

✓ To quickly create a toolbar, drag a folder from My Computer over a blank area of the taskbar and drop it.

End Task

Because the Active Desktop is a Web page, it acts as a receptacle for Web content. You can download objects (called *Active Desktop components*) from the Web, such as stock tickers and weather maps, that automatically download and display updated content right on your desktop.

Task 14: Adding Active Desktop Components from the Web

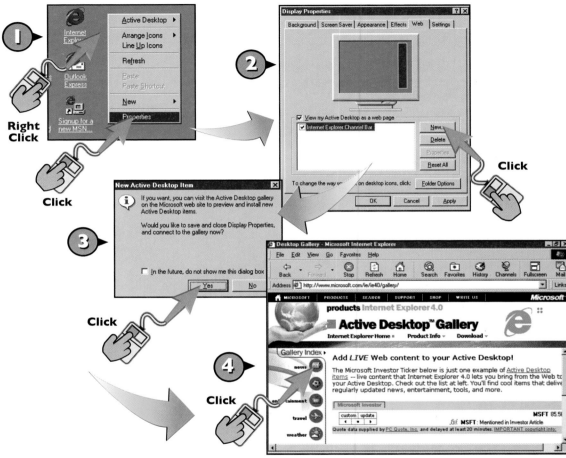

> Right-click a blank area of the Windows desktop and click **Properties**.

> Click the **Web** tab and click **New**.

> Click **Yes**.

> Internet Explorer loads the Active Desktop Gallery Web page. Follow the trail of links to the desired desktop component.

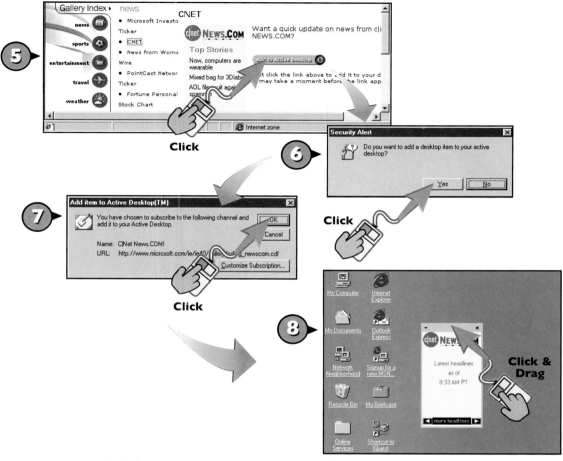

After placing a component on the desktop, you can resize or move it. Rest the mouse pointer on the top of the component to display a pop-up "title bar." Drag the bar to move the component, or drag an edge to resize it.

Click

Click

Click

Click & Drag

5 Once you've reached the component you want to add, click the **Add to Active Desktop** button.

6 When prompted to confirm, click **Yes**.

7 Internet Explorer informs you that it will set up a site subscription for the object. Click **OK**.

8 Internet Explorer places the component on the desktop. Point to the top of the component and drag the gray bar to move it.

✓ To force desktop components to download updated content, right-click a blank area of the desktop, point to **Active Desktop**, and choose **Update Now.**

End Task

Task 15: Tuning In to the Web with the Channel Bar

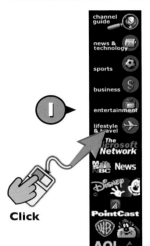

With channels, you can tune in to the best sites the Web has to offer. The **Channel** bar comes with a **Channel Finder** that allows you to select from popular sites and then place those sites on the channel changer. To view a site, you simply click a button on the channel changer.

1 Connect to the Internet and click the desired channel in the **Channel** bar on your desktop.

2 Move the mouse to the left side of the screen to bring IE4's **Channel** bar into view. Click the link for the desired Web page.

3 Click **Microsoft Channel Guide** in the **Channel** bar.

Next Step

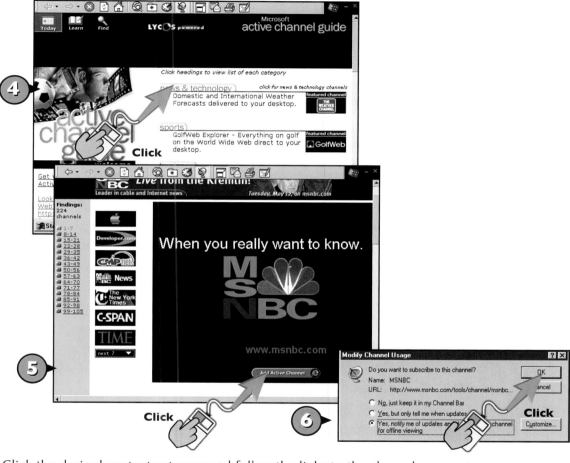

As you browse the Web, you might encounter pages that have an **Add Active Channel** link. Click the link to add the site to the **Channel bar.** You can access Microsoft's **Channel Guide** to preview additional channels and add them to the **Channel** bar.

④ ▶ Click the desired content category and follow the links to the channel you want.

⑤ ▶ Click the **Add Active Channel** link.

⑥ ▶ Enter your subscription preferences and click **OK**.

Task 16: Using the Channel Screen Saver

The Web content you can get with channels is much more dynamic than the content of standard Web pages. Many channels display content that looks like something you would see on TV or at the movies. To take advantage of this dynamic content, use the channel screen saver.

Start Here

Click

Click

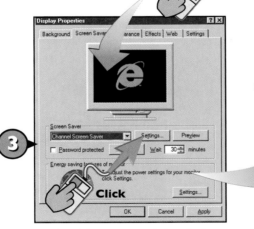

Click

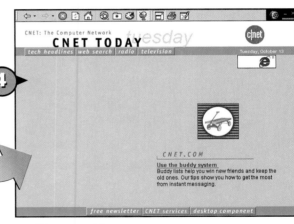

 Right-click a blank area of the desktop and choose **Properties**.

 On the **Screen Saver** tab, open the **Screen Saver** drop-down list and select **Channel Screen Saver**.

 Enter any additional settings for the screen saver and click **OK**.

 When your computer is inactive for the specified time period, the screen saver starts to display subscribed channels.

 End Task

Task 17: Adding Shortcuts for Your Favorite Web Pages

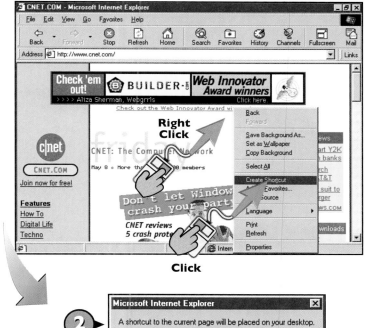

Right Click

Click

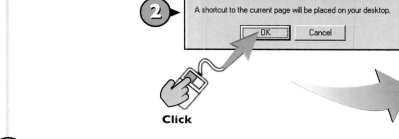

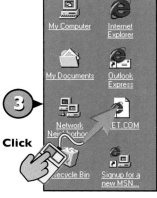

Click

Click

Click

Internet Explorer allows you to create shortcuts for your favorite Web pages and place them right on the Windows desktop. For example, you might want to add a shortcut for your local news station's Web site or for your mutual fund's Web site. To quickly open the page, you just click its shortcut.

 In Internet Explorer, right-click a blank area of the page for which you want to create a shortcut, and choose **Create Shortcut** from the ensuing menu.

 When Internet Explorer prompts you to confirm, click **OK**.

 Internet Explorer places the shortcut on the Windows desktop. Click the shortcut to open the page.

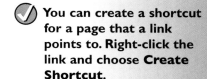 You can create a shortcut for a page that a link points to. Right-click the link and choose **Create Shortcut**.

 To place a shortcut on the **Start, Programs** menu, drag a link over the **Start** button, over **Programs**, and to the desired location.

Windows 98 comes with a collection of desktop themes that change the appearance of the Windows desktop, including the icons used for My Computer and the Recycle Bin, the mouse pointer, windows, and dialog boxes. For example, the **Dangerous Creatures** theme changes the mouse pointer into a jellyfish and displays sharks and stingrays when the screen saver starts.

Task 18: Animating Your Desktop with Desktop Themes

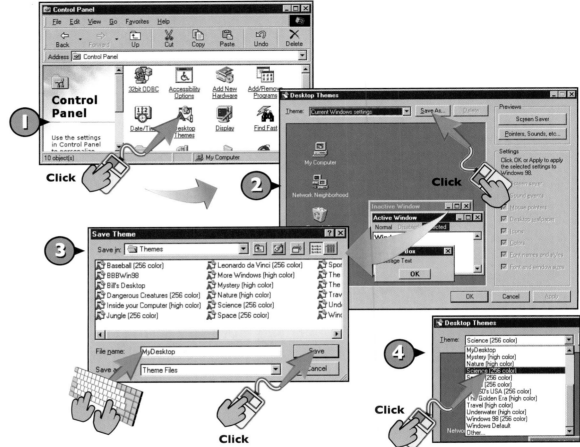

Click

Click

Click

Click

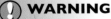

① ▶ In the Windows Control Panel, click the **Desktop Themes** icon.

② ▶ Click the **Save As** button to save your current desktop settings as a starting point.

③ ▶ Type a name for the theme in the **File name** text box, and then click the **Save** button.

④ ▶ Open the **Theme** drop-down list in the **Desktop Themes** dialog, and click the desired desktop theme.

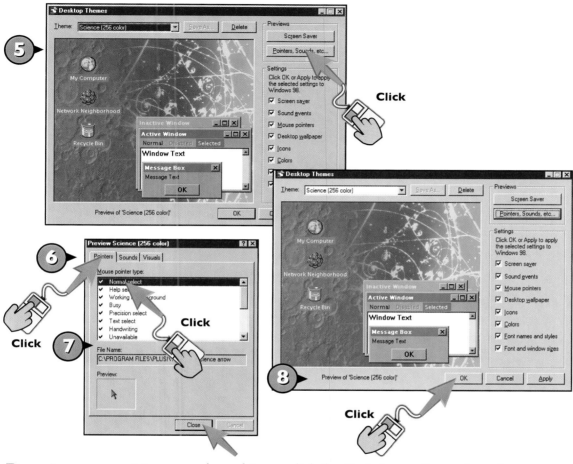

To disable a feature of the selected desktop theme, click its name to remove the check mark from its box.

WARNING
Desktop themes do require additional memory and system resources and may slightly slow down your system.

Run Windows Update, as explained in Part 1, Task 10, "Upgrading Windows with Windows Update," to check for additional desktop themes at Microsoft's Web site.

5 To preview mouse pointers, sounds, and icons, click the **Pointers, Sounds, etc.** button.

6 Click the tab for the type of object you want to preview: **Pointers**, **Sounds**, or **Visuals**.

7 Click an item in the list to display it in the preview area or double-click to play a sound. Click the **Close** button.

8 Click **OK** to save your settings.

PART 4

Configuring Outlook Express

You already know how to send and receive email messages. Now you're ready to take the next step—configuring Outlook Express. You can change its layout to make your folders more accessible, add email and news server accounts (if you use more than one), create and use an address book, retrieve messages at scheduled times, and even have incoming messages automatically routed to separate folders.

With the tasks in this part and an hour or so of free time, you'll be able to automate and optimize Outlook Express for the way you work. This part also includes a truckload of tips and tricks to help you use Outlook Express more productively.

Tasks

Task 1: Changing the Overall Layout

Outlook Express initially displays three panes: the **Outlook** bar (left), the message list (upper right), and the message preview (lower right). You can change the layout, turn on additional toolbars, move the standard toolbar, and revamp the preview pane. This task shows you just what to do.

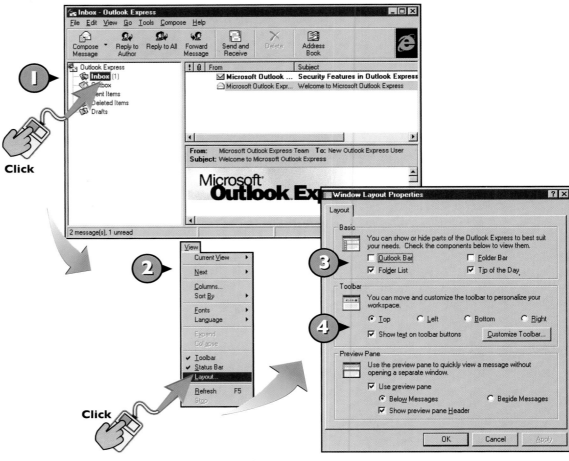

In step 3, turn off **Outlook Bar** and turn on **Folder List** to make managing your folders and messages as easy as managing folders and files in Windows Explorer.

1 ► Click the **Inbox** icon in the **Outlook** bar.

2 ► Open the **View** menu and click **Layout**.

3 ► Under **Basic**, you can turn **Outlook Bar**, **Folder List**, **Folder Bar**, and **Tip of the Day** on or off.

4 ► Under **Toolbar**, choose the desired position of the **Standard** toolbar and turn the toolbar button names on or off.

Next Step

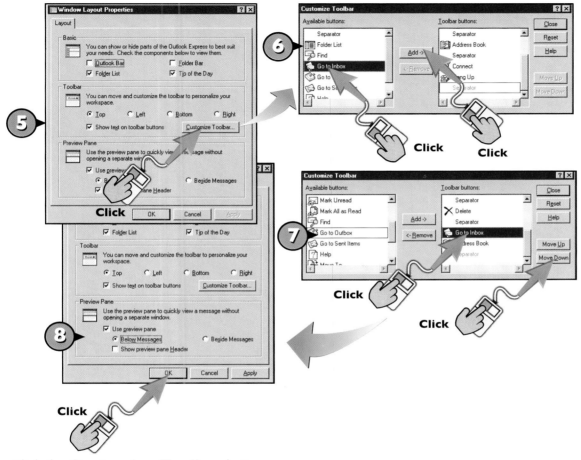

Click

WARNING
Don't clutter your screen with bars and tools you don't use. Optimize the screen area for displaying the message list and preview area.

To quickly adjust the relative size of the panes, drag the bars that separate them.

Right-click the toolbar or the **Outlook** bar to display a menu of options for configuring it.

5 ▶ Click the **Customize Toolbar** button.

6 ▶ To add a button to the toolbar, click the button's name in the **Available buttons** list and click the **Add** button.

7 ▶ To move a button, click its name in the **Toolbar buttons** list and click **Move Up** or **Move Down**. Click **Close**.

8 ▶ Enter your preferences for the preview pane (or turn it off). Click **OK** to save your changes.

End Task

Task 2: Adding a New Email Account

You probably set up an email account when you first ran Outlook Express or when you entered connection settings for your Internet service provider. But if you have changed service providers or acquired a new email account, you must enter connection settings for the new email server before you can send and receive messages.

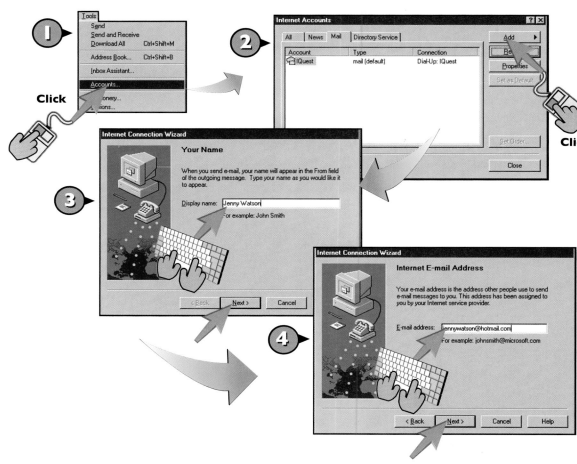

✅ If you get a new email account, you can edit the old account instead of replacing it. In step 2, instead of clicking **Add**, click the name of the existing account and click **Properties.**

① Open the **Tools** menu and click **Accounts.**

② Click the **Add** button, and click **Mail** from the ensuing list.

③ Type your name as you want it to appear on messages you send. (This can be your real name or a nickname.) Click **Next**.

④ Type your email address so people can reply to your messages. Click **Next**.

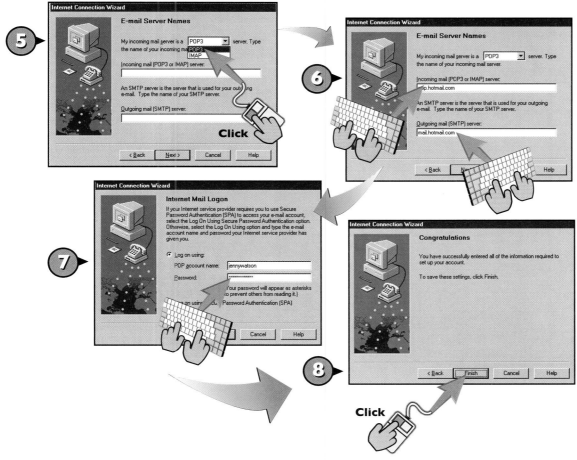

Click

Click

5 ▶ Open the drop-down list at the top of the dialog box and select the type of server used for incoming mail: **POP3** or **IMAP**.

6 ▶ Type the addresses of the incoming and outgoing mail servers as specified by your service provider. Click **Next**.

7 ▶ Enter the information required to log on to your mail server (your username and password). Click **Next**.

8 ▶ Follow the onscreen instructions to specify the type of connection you are using. Click **Finish** in the final dialog box.

✅ After you click **Finish** in step 8, you are returned to the **Internet Accounts** dialog box. Click the email account you want to use as the default account and click **Set as Default**. Click **Close**.

✅ If you cancel an email account, you can delete it. Choose **Tools, Accounts**, click the **Mail** tab, click the account's name, and click **Remove**.

Task 3: Adding a Newsgroup Account

The typical Internet service provider news server provides access to more than 20,000 newsgroups, but may not subscribe to specialized newsgroups, such as Microsoft's newsgroups. You can set up a new newsgroup account to access these newsgroups.

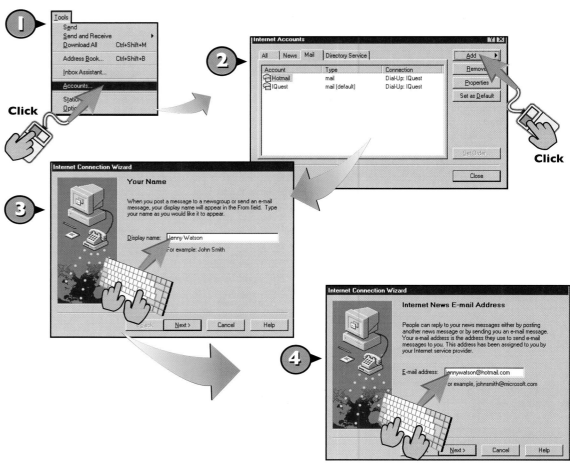

✓ Use IE4 to pull up a list of public news servers from **in-motion.net/ publicnntp.html**. Or use your favorite Web search tool to search for **public news server.**

① ▶ Open the **Tools** menu and click **Accounts**.

② ▶ Click the **Add** button, and click **News** from the ensuing list.

③ ▶ Type your name as you want it to appear on messages you post. (This can be your real name or a nickname.) Click **Next**.

④ ▶ Type your email address so that people can reply to you privately, via email. Click **Next**.

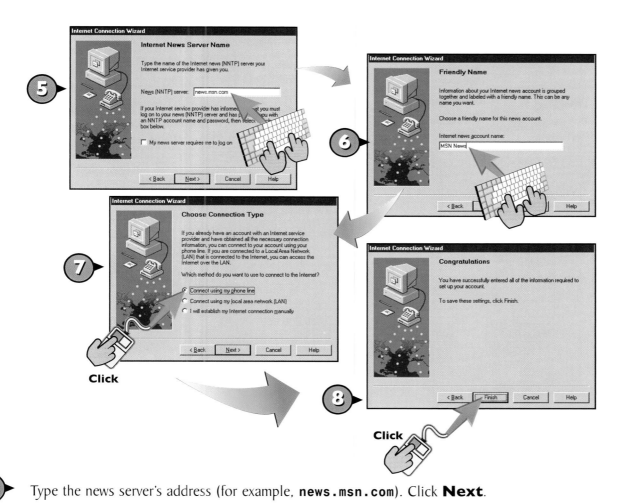

5 Type the news server's address (for example, **news.msn.com**). Click **Next**.

6 Type a descriptive name for this account. Click **Next**.

7 Follow the onscreen instructions to specify your connection type and enter your name and password (if required).

8 Click **Finish**.

After you click **Finish** in step 8, you are returned to the **Internet Accounts** dialog box. Click the newsgroup account you want to use as the default account and click **Set as Default**. Click **Close**.

WARNING
Some public news servers require you to log on. Contact the news server administrator to determine the username and password to use.

Task 4: Accessing Outlook's Options Dialog Box

Most of Outlook Express' configuration settings are accessible via the Options dialog box. Here, you will find options for sending and receiving messages, making Outlook Express your default email program, and having Outlook Express automatically download messages. These steps show you how to display and navigate the dialog box. Additional tasks in this part show how to enter specific settings.

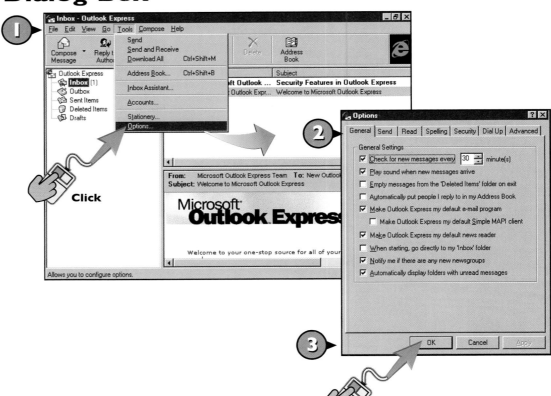

Click

Click

 Open the **Tools** menu and choose **Options**.

 Click the tab for the options you want to change and enter your changes.

 Click **OK**.

Task 5: Entering General Preferences

Start Here

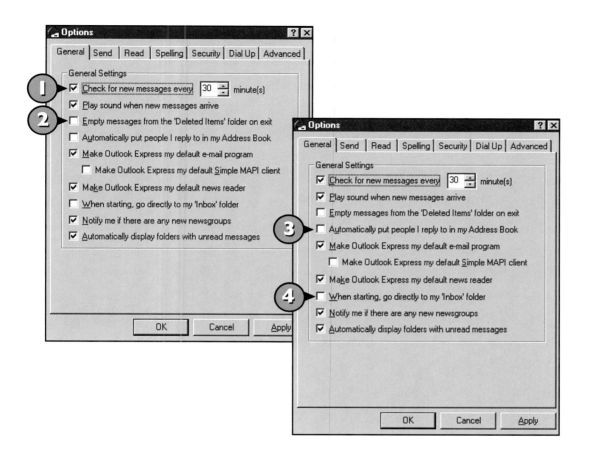

The **General** tab offers options that can save you a great deal of time, including settings for having Outlook Express add the names and addresses of the people you correspond with to the **Address Book** and automatically displaying the contents of the Inbox on startup. These steps show you how to enter your preferences.

✓ To run Outlook Express from Internet Explorer, see Part 2, Task 14, "Running Outlook Express from Internet Explorer."

⚠ **WARNING**
If you set up Outlook Express to check for messages, Outlook Express may dial when you don't want it to. If you are billed for every minute of Internet connect time, consider turning off this option.

1 ▶ On the **General** tab of the **Options** dialog, turn on **Check for new messages every ___ minute(s)** and enter the desired number of minutes.

2 ▶ To save disk space, turn on **Empty messages from the 'Deleted Items' folder on exit**.

3 ▶ To automate your address book, turn on **Automatically put people I reply to in my Address Book**.

4 ▶ To display received messages when Outlook Express starts, turn on **When starting, go directly to my 'Inbox' folder**.

End Task

Task 6: Controlling How Messages Are Sent

When you click the **Compose Message** button or choose to reply to a message, the message window appears, prompting you to address and compose the message. Although you may not realize it, you can control the appearance of this window and the way it functions.

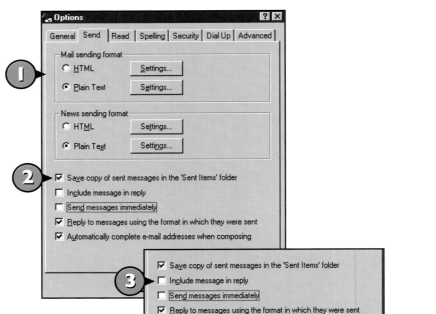

To change the format setting for a message you are composing, open the **Format** menu in the **New Message** window and choose **Rich Text (HTML)** or **Plain Text**.

 In the **Send** tab of the **Options** dialog box, choose the desired format for messages: **HTML** or **Plain Text**.

 To keep a copy of messages you send, turn on **Save copy of sent messages in the 'Sent Items' folder**.

 To prevent Outlook Express from quoting the original message in your reply, turn off **Include message in reply**.

 To compose messages offline and send them later (only when you click **Send and Receive**), turn off **Send messages immediately**.

Task 7: Controlling How Messages Are Received

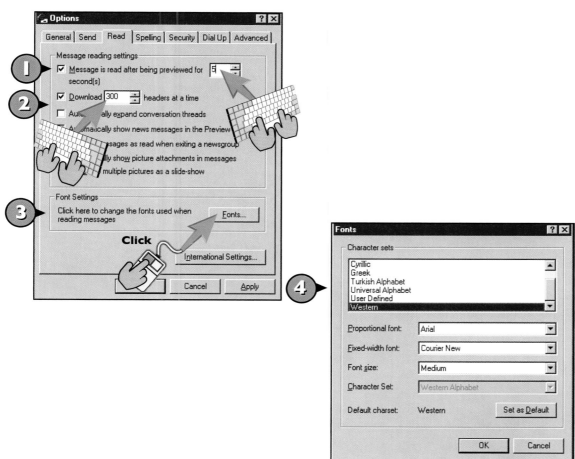

In addition to controlling the way **Outlook Express** handles outgoing messages, you can control the way **Outlook Express** manages the messages you receive. These steps show you how to enter the most common settings. (Most of the options deal with newsgroup messages.)

In the **Read** tab of the **Options** dialog box, type the number of seconds you want Outlook Express to wait before marking a highlighted message as "read."

Enter the maximum number of message headers (descriptions) you want Outlook Express to download at one time.

Click the **Fonts** button.

Choose the desired type style and size for displaying message contents, and click **OK**.

 When you highlight a message description, Outlook Express assumes that you are reading the message and changes the description from bold to normal, indicating that you've read the message.

End Task

Task 8: Entering Spelling Checker Preferences

Start Here

Outlook Express has a built-in spelling checker that can help you eliminate typos and misspellings from your messages. Before sending a message, choose **Tools, Spelling** to run the spelling checker. These steps show you how to enter preferences to control the way the spelling checker does its job.

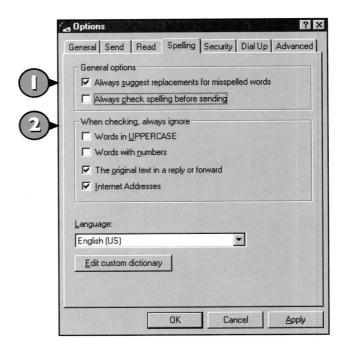

✓ To create a supplemental dictionary so the spelling checker won't stop on special terms you use, click **Edit custom dictionary**, type the terms, and save the dictionary.

1 In the **Spelling** tab of the **Options** dialog box, check **Always check spelling before sending**.

2 Choose which text strings you want the spelling checker to ignore, and click **OK**.

Task 9: Setting Up Outlook Express to Autodial

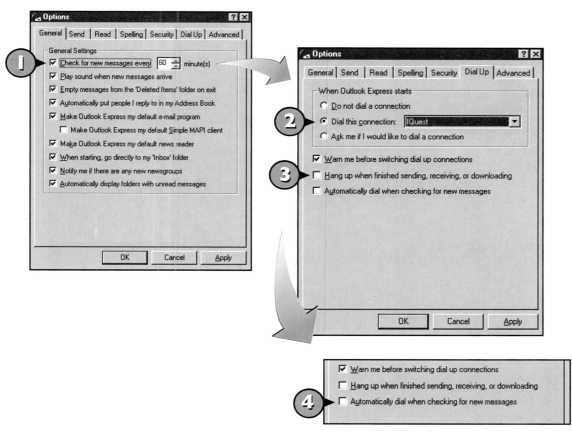

If you find yourself frequently clicking the **Send and Receive** button to check for new messages, consider making Outlook Express automatically check for messages.

In the **General** tab of the **Options** dialog box, make sure **Check for new messages every ___ minutes** is on.

Click the **Dial Up** tab, click **Dial this connection**, and choose the desired connection (if you have more than one).

To have Outlook Express disconnect after retrieving email, turn on **Hang up when finished sending, receiving, or downloading**.

To connect automatically when you click the **Send and Receive** button, turn on **Automatically dial when checking for new messages**.

✓ If you turn on **Hang up when finished sending** in step 3, Outlook Express sends mail from the **Outbox**, retrieves mail, and then disconnects. To remain connected, turn off this option.

Task 10: Cleaning Up Your Message Folders

As you send and receive email and newsgroup messages, Outlook Express dutifully stores the messages in the **Inbox** and **Sent Items** folders, occupying precious disk space. You should do a little housekeeping regularly to reclaim this space.

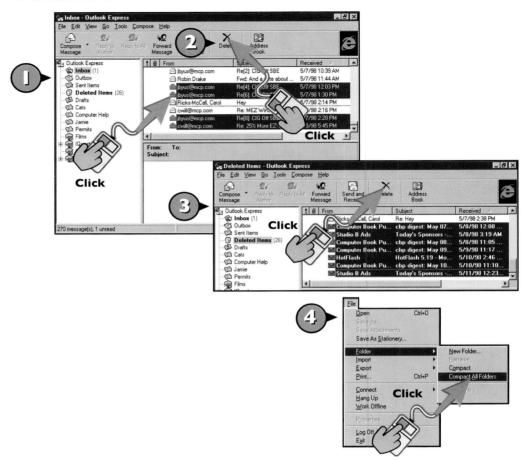

✓ You may need to retain certain messages for legal and professional purposes or to keep a record of the email addresses of friends, relatives, colleagues, and clients.

✓ You can drag messages from one folder to another. To undelete messages, drag them from the **Deleted Items** folder to another folder.

 Click a message to select it. **Ctrl+click** or **Shift+click** to select multiple messages.

 Click the **Delete** button (or press the **Delete** key) to move the messages to the **Deleted Items** folder.

 To delete messages permanently, select them in the **Deleted Items** folder and click the **Delete** button.

 To reclaim disk space left by deleted messages, open the **File** menu, point to **Folder**, and click **Compact All Folders**.

Task 11: Sorting Messages

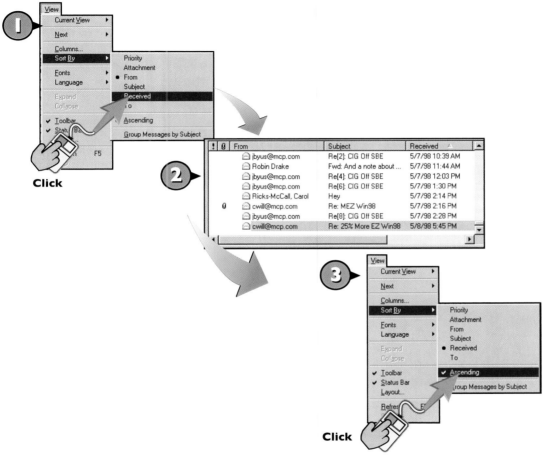

Click

Click

If your **Inbox** or **Sent Items** folder is packed with messages, tracking down a message you received last week (or last year) can be tough. To help, you can have Outlook Express sort the messages by date, sender, recipient, or subject.

1. Open the **View** menu, point to **Sort By**, and choose the desired sort option (for example, choose **Received** to sort by date).

2. Outlook Express rearranges the messages; in this case, messages are sorted by date in ascending order (oldest messages first).

3. To reverse the sort order, open the **View** menu, point to **Sort By**, and click **Ascending**.

✅ Click a column heading to sort the message list using the entries in that column. Click the heading again to reverse the sort order.

✅ To track down a specific message, choose **Edit, Find Message**.

Task 12: Creating a New Message Folder

Do you find yourself frequently using the **Sort** feature to track down messages from a specific person or about a specific topic? Then consider creating folders for storing related messages. These steps show you how to create your own folders.

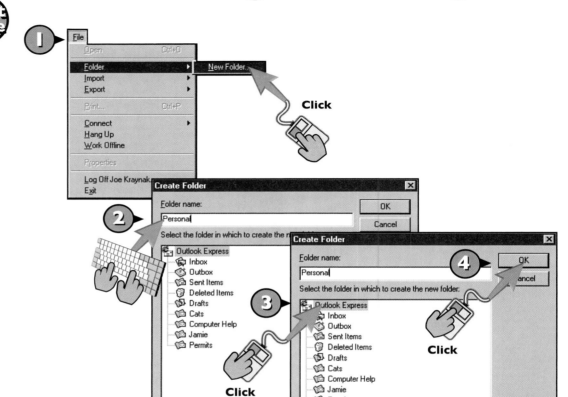

✓ To create a folder that's on the same level as the rest of the folders, choose the topmost folder in the list.

✓ You can easily move messages by dragging them from the message list and dropping them onto a folder or icon in the left pane.

1 ▶ Open the **File** menu, point to **Folder**, and choose **New Folder**.

2 ▶ Type a name for the folder.

3 ▶ Choose the existing folder in which you want the new subfolder placed.

4 ▶ Click **OK**.

Task 13: Filtering Messages with Inbox Assistant

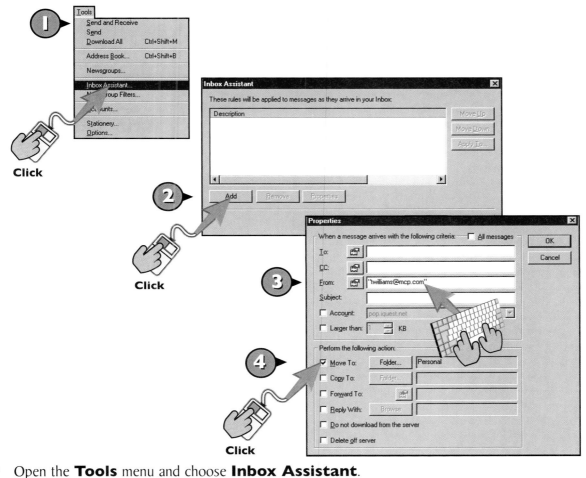

Click

Click

Click

If you find yourself frequently moving messages from the **Inbox** to a different folder, consider creating a *mail filter*. The filter automatically routes incoming messages to a specific folder based on the **From** or **Subject** entries. Outlook Express features the Inbox Assistant for setting up filters.

Open the **Tools** menu and choose **Inbox Assistant**.

Click the **Add** button.

Click in the **From** or **Subject** text box and type an entry (in quotes) to specify what you want the filter to look for.

Click **Move To**, choose the desired folder, and click **OK**.

The Inbox Assistant can also automatically forward messages to another email address, send automatic replies, and more.

Task 14: Creating an Email Address Book

Email addresses can be quite long and difficult to remember. To help, you can create your own email address book. You can enter in it the names and addresses of your friends, relatives, colleagues, and customers, and never have to worry about misplacing an address again!

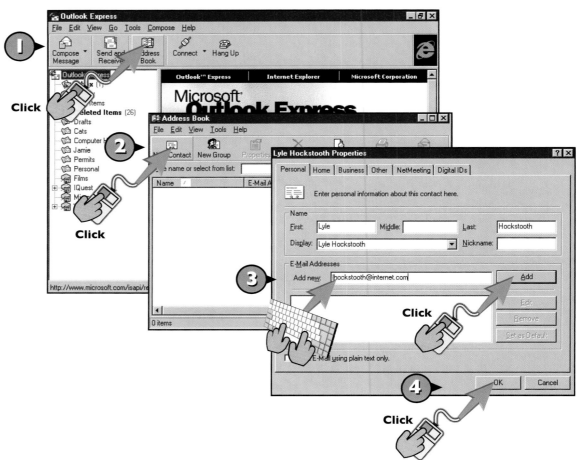

✓ To make it easier to recognize people in the address book, type the person's name in the **Display** text box. This makes the entry more personal.

1 ▶ Click the **Address Book** button.

2 ▶ Click the **New Contact** button.

3 ▶ Enter the person's name and email address in the appropriate text boxes and click the **Add** button.

4 ▶ Click **OK**.

Next Step

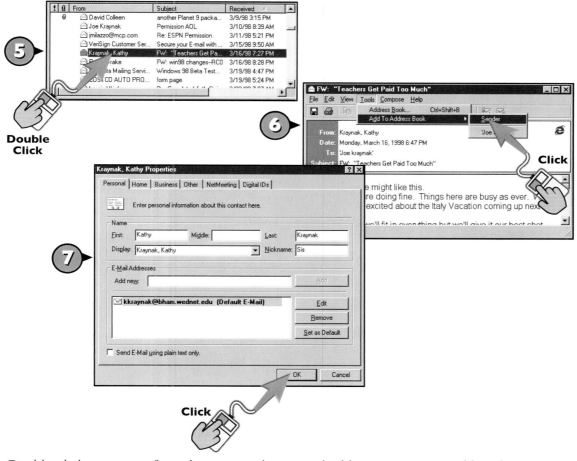

Double Click

Click

Click

Although you can click the
New Contact button and
type names and addresses
into your address book,
there is another, faster way
to add entries. These steps
show you how.

5 Double-click a message from the person whose email address you want to add to the address book.

6 Open the **Tools** menu, point to **Add To Address Book**, and click **Sender**.

7 Enter additional information about the person (if desired) and click **OK**.

 To make a mailing list, click the **New Group** or **New List** button and add recipients to the group.

 End Task

Task 15: Inserting Email Addresses from the Address Book

When composing a message, you can insert the recipient's email address from the address book without having to type it.

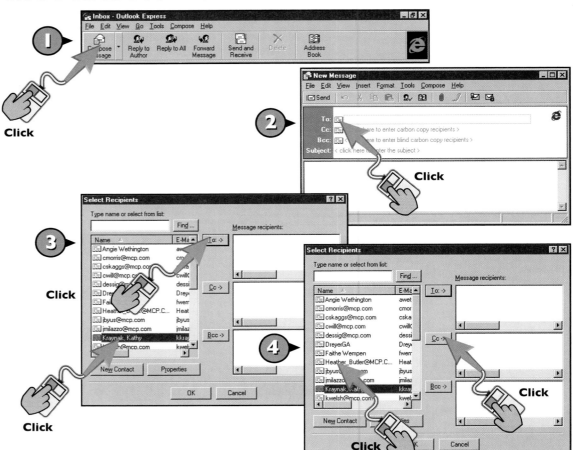

Click

Click

Click

Click

Click

Click

✓ To quickly add a person's name to the **Recipients** list, double-click the name.

1 ▶ Click the **Compose Message** button.

2 ▶ Click the card icon next to **To**.

3 ▶ Click the name of the person to whom you want to send the message and click the **To** button.

4 ▶ To send a copy of the message to someone else, click the person's name and click the **Cc** button.

Next
Step

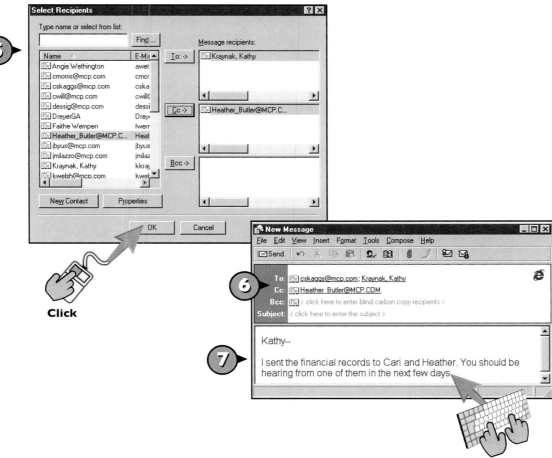

Click

5 Click **OK**.

6 If you chose to send the message to two or more people, their names (or email addresses) appear in the **To** field, separated by semicolons.

7 Compose and send the message as you normally would.

✓ Not sure whom to write to? Click the **Address Book** button in the Outlook Express window. Right-click the person's name and choose **Send Mail**.

✓ Instead of clicking the card next to **To**, click in the **To** field and start typing the person's name or email address. Outlook Express automatically completes the entry.

PART

Task 16: Finding People's Email Addresses

The Internet has several online email and phone directories you can use to find email addresses. The Outlook Express address book offers a feature that lets you search the most popular directories by entering the name of the person whose email address you're looking for.

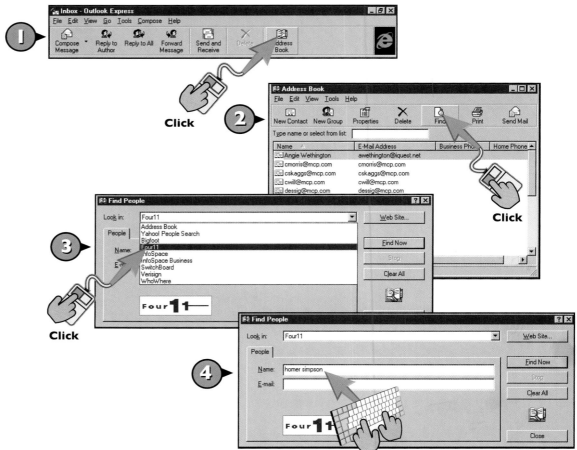

Click

Click

Click

Click

✓ If your search turns up nothing, try to broaden the search by typing only the person's last name.

1 ▶ Click the **Address Book** button.

2 ▶ Click the **Find** button (or press **Ctrl+F**).

3 ▶ Open the **Look in** drop-down list and choose the directory you want to search.

4 ▶ Click in the **Name** text box and type the person's first and last name.

Next Step

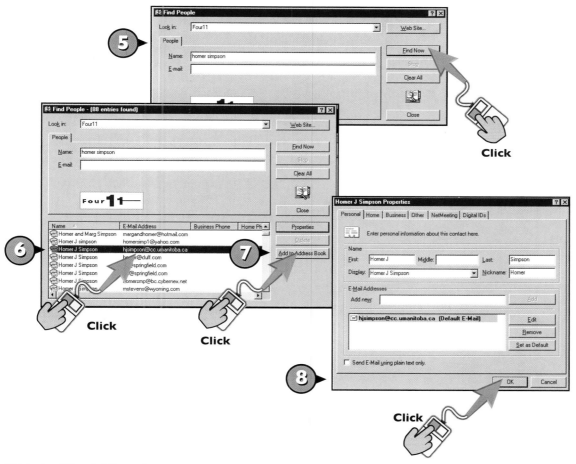

Click

Click

Click

Click

5 Click the **Find Now** button.

6 In the list of entries that your search generated, click the desired entry.

7 Click the **Add to Address Book** button.

8 Enter additional information about the person (if desired) and click **OK**.

To find out more
information or to refine
your search, use Internet
Explorer to access the
Web versions of these
directories:

www.four11.com
www.bigfoot.com
www.infospace.com
www.whowhere.com

PART 5

Using Windows 98 on a Notebook PC

More and more people are replacing their desktop PC dinosaurs with sleek notebook computers that not only weigh less but also outperform low-end desktop PCs. Most notebook PCs are equipped with 32MB of RAM, a 2GB hard disk, a CD-ROM drive, a sound card, and several ports and expansion slots for installing additional equipment. In addition, many manufacturers offer docking stations into which you can plug your notebook PC to give it a full-size monitor and keyboard as well as other amenities you would find only in a desktop model.

To keep up with these powerful new portable computers, Windows includes many features designed specifically for notebook computers, including plug-and-play support for PCMCIA cards, enhanced power-saving features, and a Briefcase utility for quickly transferring files from your notebook to your desktop PC. In this part, you will learn how to use these features to harness the power of your notebook computer.

Tasks

Notebook PCs make it easy to upgrade by using **PCMCIA** cards (PC cards, for short). *PCMCIA* stands for Personal Computer Memory Card International Association, an organization that has developed a set of standards for small devices that plug directly into expansion slots on the *outside* of the computer. These cards are about the size of credit cards, and you can insert them when the power is on.

⚠ WARNING
Don't remove a PC card before disabling it. The steps on the facing page show how to safely remove a PC card when the power is on.

✓ If your notebook PC has two empty slots, typically marked 0 and 1, use the number 0 (top) slot first.

Task 1: Adding and Removing PC (PCMCIA) Cards

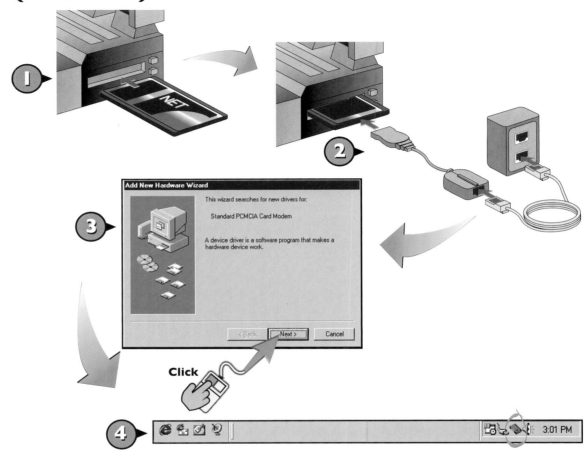

Click

① Turn on your computer and insert the PC card (label up) into one of the PCMCIA slots on your computer.

② If the card requires you to connect a cable or phone line, plug the cable or phone line into the opening on the card.

③ If this is the first time you've inserted the card, Windows runs the Add New Hardware wizard. Follow the wizard's instructions.

④ The system tray (on the right end of the taskbar) displays an icon for your PCMCIA sockets.

Next Step

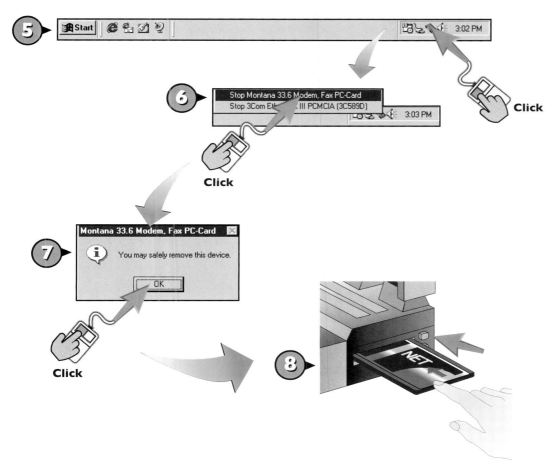

Click

Click

Click

To prevent damage to a PC card, you should disable it before removing it. This cuts the power to the PC card, so you can safely remove it. The PC Card utility allows you to quickly disable a card, as shown here.

⚠ WARNING
To avoid damaging your notebook PC or PCMCIA card, check the manufacturer's documentation to determine whether it is safe to exchange cards while your system is running.

✓ When you insert or remove a PC card, Windows emits a two-toned beep to indicate that the card has been successfully inserted or removed.

5 Click the **PC Card (PCMCIA) Status** icon in the system tray.

6 Click the **Stop...** option for the card you want to remove.

7 A dialog box appears, indicating that it is safe to remove the card. Click **OK**.

8 Press the Eject button next to the PC card and remove the card.

Task 2: Plugging In to a Docking Station

A docking station or *port replicator* is a unit that contains ports for a monitor, printer, keyboard, mouse, speakers, and other devices. You plug your notebook PC into the docking station so you can use your notebook PC as a desktop PC. To use a docking station, you must create a separate hardware profile for the docked and undocked state, as shown in these steps.

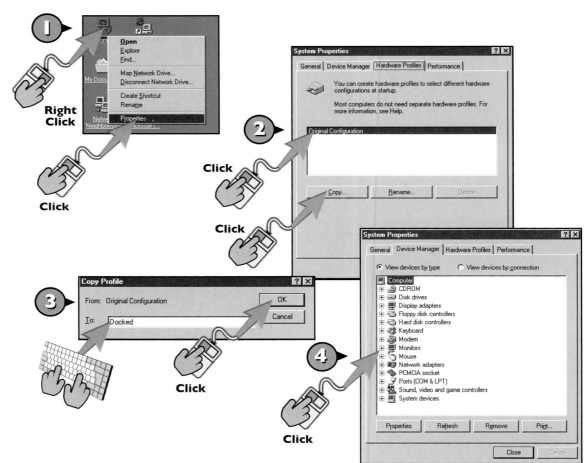

WARNING

To protect your notebook PC and docking station, turn off the power before docking. On some units this may not be necessary.

1 Right-click **My Computer** and choose **Properties**.

2 On the **Hardware Profiles** tab, click **Original Configuration** and then click the **Copy** button.

3 Type **Docked** as the name of your new configuration and click **OK**.

4 On the **Device Manager** tab, click the plus sign next to a device you want disabled when the notebook is docked.

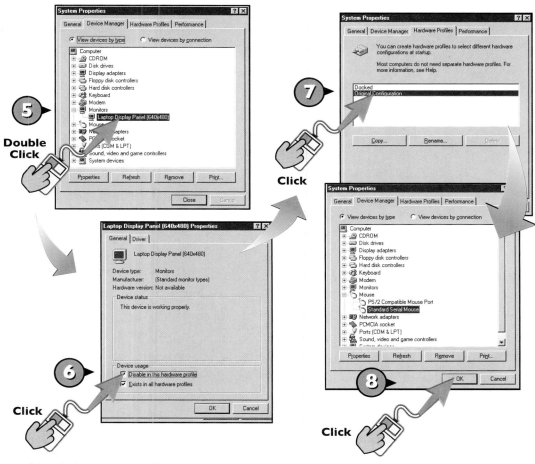

Double Click

Click

Click

Click

5 Double-click the name of the device you want to disable.

6 Click **Disable in this hardware profile**, and click **OK**.

7 On the **Hardware Profiles** tab, choose **Original Configuration**.

8 Repeat steps 4 through 7 to disable all devices connected to the docking station. Click **OK**.

✓ If the notebook PC did not come with a docking station option, it may have ports for connecting a monitor, keyboard, and mouse.

✓ To learn more about creating hardware profiles and disabling devices, see Part 1, Task 15, "Using Different Hardware Profiles."

✓ If Windows can't determine which hardware profile to use on startup, it displays a list of profiles from which you can choose.

End Task

Task 3: Taking Work on the Road with Briefcase

If you have both a notebook and desktop computer, you might need to transfer files from your desktop computer to your notebook computer to take work on the road. To expedite this process and avoid replacing newer versions of your files with older versions, use Briefcase.

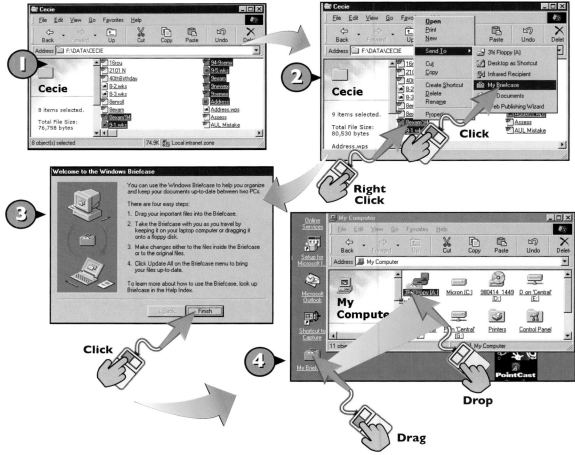

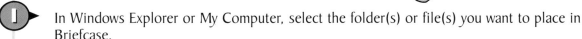

1 ▶ In Windows Explorer or My Computer, select the folder(s) or file(s) you want to place in Briefcase.

2 ▶ Right-click one of the selected items, point to **Send To**, and click **My Briefcase**.

3 ▶ If the **Welcome to the Windows Briefcase** dialog box appears, click **Finish** to copy the selected items to your Briefcase.

4 ▶ Insert a blank disk into the floppy disk drive and then drag and drop the **My Briefcase** icon over the floppy disk icon.

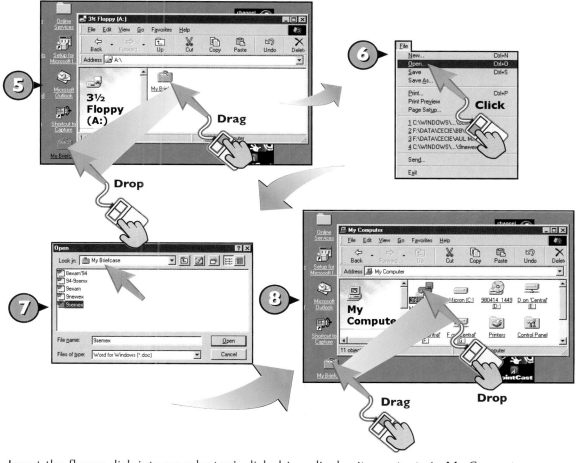

When you're on the road, insert the floppy disk that contains the contents of My Briefcase into your notebook PC's floppy disk drive, and then copy Briefcase to the Windows desktop. You can then open files from My Briefcase and edit them.

5 Insert the floppy disk into your laptop's disk drive, display its contents in My Computer, and drag and drop the **My Briefcase** icon onto the Windows desktop.

6 To open a file from Briefcase, run the program you want to use to open the file and choose its **File**, **Open** command.

7 Open the **Look in** drop-down list, choose **My Briefcase**, and open the document file as you normally would.

8 When you are ready to end your trip, drag and drop the **My Briefcase** icon onto the icon for your floppy disk.

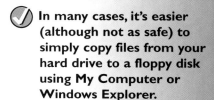

In many cases, it's easier (although not as safe) to simply copy files from your hard drive to a floppy disk using My Computer or Windows Explorer.

End Task

Task 4: Returning the Briefcase to Your Desktop PC

When you return from your trip, you'll need to copy the edited document files from your notebook **PC** to your desktop **PC.** You do this by dragging the **My Briefcase** icon from the floppy disk to the Windows desktop on the desktop **PC. My Briefcase** will let you know which files need to be updated.

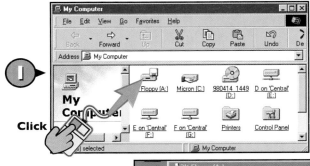

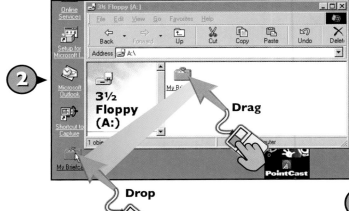

 You can also transfer files between a notebook and desktop computer by connecting the parallel or serial ports on the two computers with a special cable, as explained in Part 6, Task 6, "Setting Up a Direct Cable Connection Between Two Computers."

 Insert the floppy disk into your desktop PC's floppy drive and click the floppy drive's icon in My Computer.

 Drag the **My Briefcase** icon over to the Windows desktop and release the mouse button.

 Click the **My Briefcase** icon to display its contents.

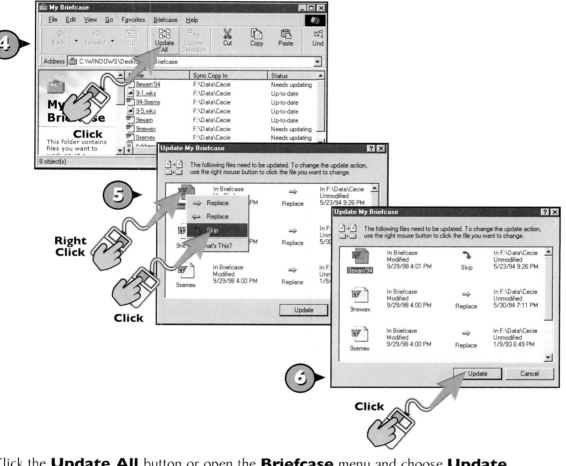

My Briefcase displays a list of document files, which shows the dates on which the files were last modified. This helps you decide which files you can safely replace.

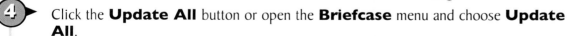

4 ▶ Click the **Update All** button or open the **Briefcase** menu and choose **Update All**.

5 ▶ If desired, you can prevent a file from being updated by right-clicking it and choosing **Skip**.

6 ▶ After marking any files you want to skip, click the **Update** button.

Task 5: Connecting to Your Office PC Via Modem

Start Here

When you're on the road with your notebook PC, you can "call" your desktop PC via modem and connect to it using Dial-Up Networking. You can then copy files and run programs from your desktop computer or network server. To perform this task, first work through Part 6, Task 1, "Installing the Network Hardware," and Tasks 4 through 9.

✓ When setting up Dial-Up Networking to share resources between computers via modem, you set up your notebook PC as the *client* and the desktop PC as the *server*. The client can then request files and have the server deliver them.

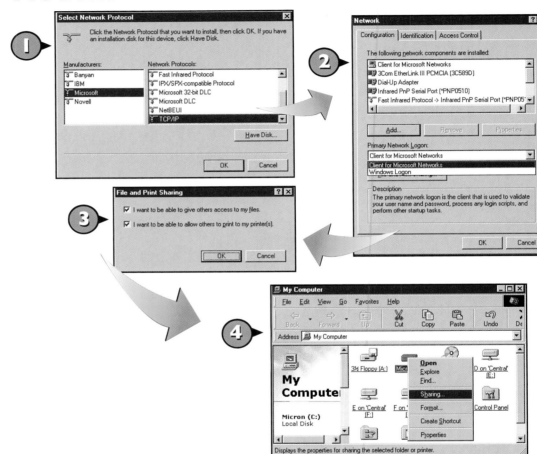

1 On both computers, install the TCP/IP network protocol, as explained in Part 6, Task 4.

2 On the notebook PC, make sure **Primary Network Logon** is set as **Client for Microsoft Networks**, as explained in Part 6, Task 7.

3 Set up file and printer sharing on your desktop PC, as explained in Part 6, Task 6.

4 On the desktop computer, enter share settings for any disks or folders you want to be able to access (see Part 6, Task 9).

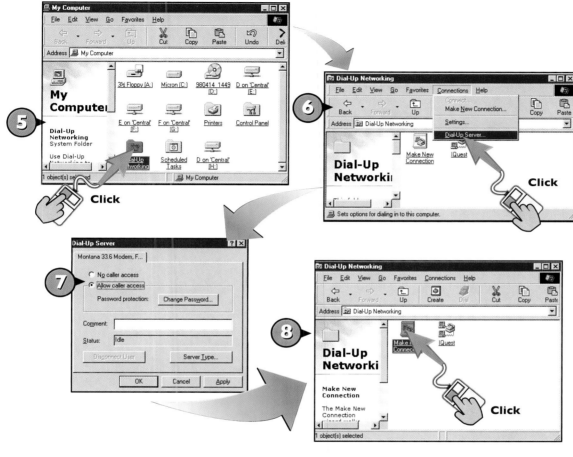

These steps show you how to create a Dial-Up Networking icon for dialing into your desktop computer. Leave your desktop computer on when you take your trip. When you're ready to connect, click the new **Dial-Up Networking** icon on your notebook PC. You can then share resources, as explained in Part 6, Task 9.

5 On the desktop PC, open My Computer and click the **Dial-Up Networking** icon.

6 Open the **Connections** menu and choose **Dial-Up Server**.

7 Turn on **Allow caller access** and specify a password, if desired. Click **OK**. (A **Dial-Up Server** icon appears in the system tray.)

8 On your notebook computer, run Dial-Up Networking, click the **Make New Connection** icon, and follow the instructions.

Task 6: Using an Infrared (Wireless) Connection

Most notebook PCs have a built-in infrared (IRdA) port, which allows you to connect wireless infrared devices to the PC. These devices include keyboards, mice, joysticks, printers, and even network connections.

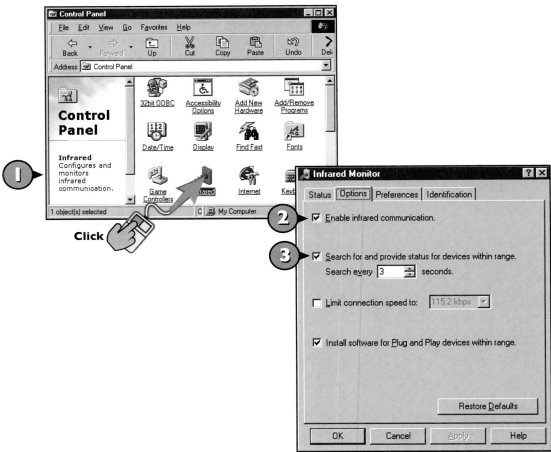

Click

✓ Infrared connections work like TV remote controls. For the connection to work, there must be a direct line of sight between the two devices.

✓ Infrared peripherals are not very popular. Check computer magazines and mail order companies.

1 ▶ In the Control Panel, click the **Infrared** icon.

2 ▶ In the **Options** tab of the **Infrared Monitor** dialog, place a check mark in the **Enable infrared communication** check box.

3 ▶ Place a check mark in the **Search for and provide status for devices within range** check box.

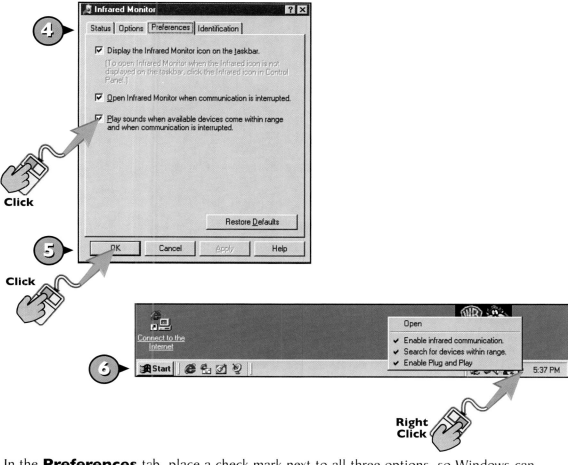

Windows 98 supports infrared ports and includes a utility called Infrared Monitor that can help you manage your infrared devices and troubleshoot common problems.

Click

Click

Right Click

 In the **Preferences** tab, place a check mark next to all three options, so Windows can notify you of the status of your infrared connections.

 Click **OK**.

 Right-click the **Infrared Monitor** icon in the system tray to view infrared communications options.

Task 7: Conserving Battery Power

Any computer is only as good as its power source. If the power fails, you lose data and have to restart your programs hoping that no critical files were damaged. On a notebook PC running on batteries, power is even less reliable, so you must manage it well and have some way of knowing when the power is running out.

For additional instructions on changing the power settings, see Part 1, Tasks 13, "Adjusting the Power-Management Settings," and 21, "Checking Your Computer's Power-Saving Features."

⊘ WARNING
Check your notebook PC's documentation to determine whether its built-in power-saving features will conflict with the Windows power-saving features.

Click

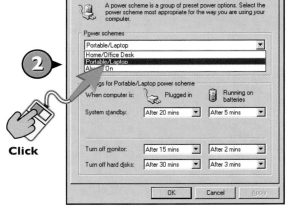

Click

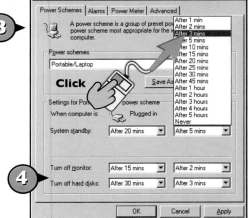

Click

In the Windows Control Panel, click the **Power Management** icon.

Open the **Power schemes** drop-down list and choose **Portable/Laptop**.

Under **Running on batteries**, open the **System standby** drop-down list and choose the desired period of inactivity before you PC goes into Standby mode.

Under **Running on batteries**, choose the desired settings for automatically shutting down the monitor and hard disk drive.

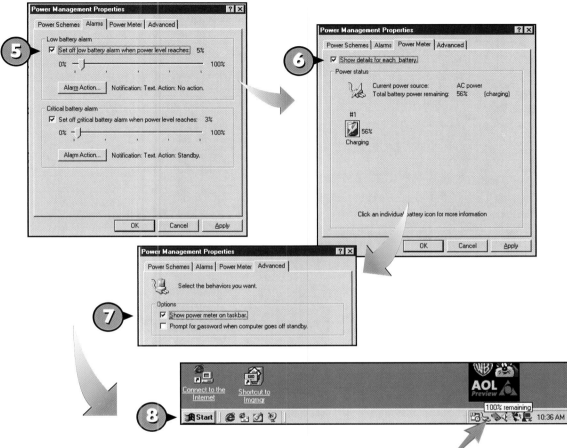

Windows features a power meter that can keep you constantly informed of how much power your battery has left along with alarms to inform you when the power is running low.

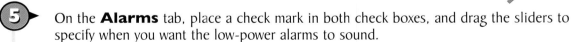

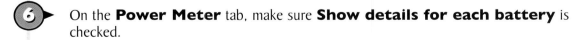

5 ▸ On the **Alarms** tab, place a check mark in both check boxes, and drag the sliders to specify when you want the low-power alarms to sound.

6 ▸ On the **Power Meter** tab, make sure **Show details for each battery** is checked.

7 ▸ On the **Advanced** tab, make sure **Show power meter on taskbar** is checked. Click **OK**.

8 ▸ Point to the **Power Meter** icon at any time to view the status of your battery power.

Task 8: Deferring Printing When Not Connected to a Printer

Unless you shelled out $300 for a portable printer, you don't have printing capabilities when you take work on the road. However, you can still print documents *offline* in Windows and then print those documents when you return to your home or office.

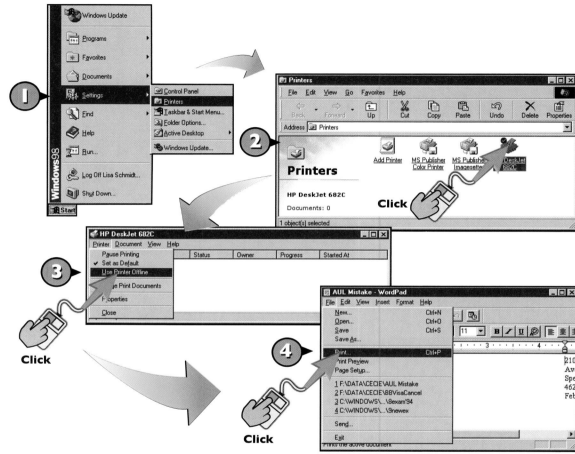

Start Here

Click

Click

Click

Click

✓ A quicker way to place your printer in offline mode is to right-click your printer's icon and choose **Use Printer Offline**.

1 ▶ Choose **Start**, **Settings**, **Printers**.

2 ▶ Click the icon for the printer you want to use.

3 ▶ Open the **Printer** menu and click **Use Printer Offline**.

4 ▶ Print the documents as you normally would.

Next Step ▶

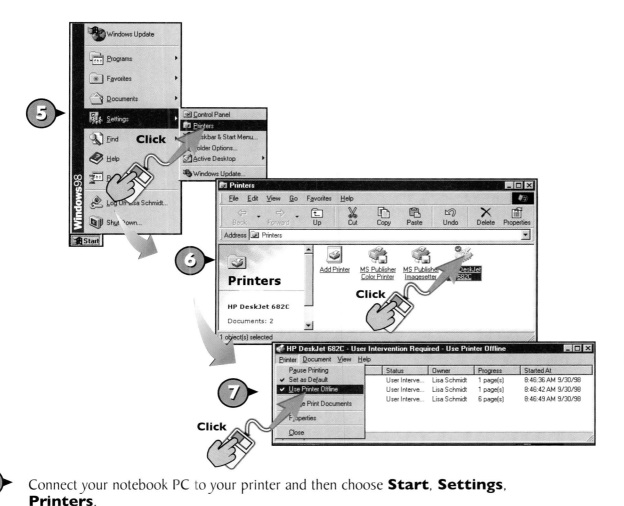

When you print a
document offline, it is saved
to your notebook PC's hard
disk. When you connect the
PC to a printer and turn off
Use Printer Offline,
Windows sends the
document to the printer.

(5) Connect your notebook PC to your printer and then choose **Start**, **Settings**,
Printers.

(6) Click the icon for the printer you chose to use for offline printing.

(7) Open the **Printer** menu and click **Use Printer Offline** to turn it off. Windows
sends the document(s) to the printer.

To defer printing on a
desktop PC, click your
printer icon and then open
the **File** menu and choose
Pause Printing. Print the
documents and then
choose **File, Pause
Printing** again when
you're ready to print.

WARNING
When connecting or
disconnecting a computer
and printer, make sure the
power is off on both
devices.

The built-in pointing devices on notebook PCs are horrible. Touchpads are too sensitive and unpredictable, and trackballs make it tough to drag and drop. The solution is to disable the built-in device and install a standard mouse. These steps show you what to do.

✅ On most systems, you can use the mouse and touchpad together.

Task 9: Attaching a Mouse to Your Notebook PC

Start Here

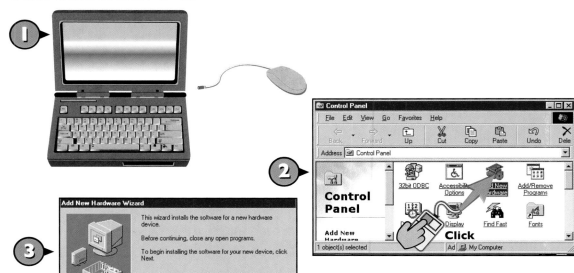

 With the power off, plug your mouse into the mouse port or serial port and then turn on your computer.

 If Windows does not detect the device, open the Control Panel and click **Add New Hardware**.

 Follow the Add New Hardware wizard's instructions to install the mouse driver.

 In the Control Panel, click the **System** icon.

Next Step

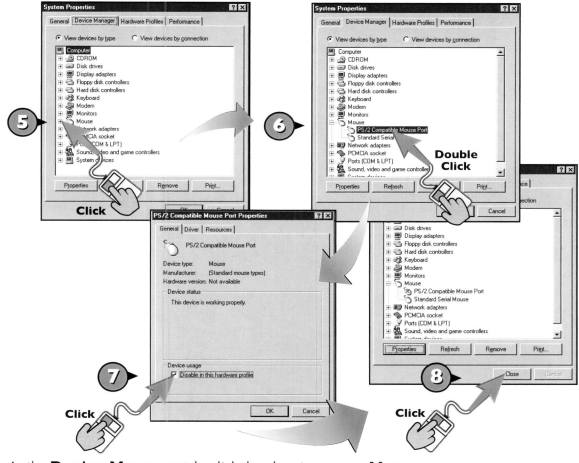

Although touchpads are nifty devices, they can cause problems as you type. Even if you crank the sensitivity down, any slight tap from your thumb can send the mouse pointer across the screen or select an option you did not wish to select. Consider disabling the touchpad, as shown here.

Click

Double Click

Click

Click

In the **Device Manager** tab, click the plus sign next to **Mouse**.

Double-click the driver for your touchpad.

Check the **Disable in this hardware profile** option and click **OK**.

Click **Close** to save your settings and then restart Windows if prompted to do so.

✓ Create two hardware profiles—one for the mouse and one for the touchpad. See Part 1, Task 15, "Using Different Hardware Profiles."

✓ You may also be able to disable the touchpad in your computer's BIOS setup. See Part 1, Tasks 17 through 21.

End Task

Setting Up and Using a Network

Corporations and even some small businesses connect their computers using special network cables to enable personnel to share equipment, resources, and data. The network allows people to connect to a central computer called the network server or to connect directly to other computers on a peer-to-peer network. It also saves the company money by allowing several people to use an expensive piece of equipment, such as an optical disc drive (for data storage) or a high-end printer.

Windows has built-in network support that provides the tools you need to set up a simple network and use it to share resources. The tasks in this part show you how to set up and manage a peer-to-peer network using the Windows 98 networking tools.

Tasks

To create a network using only two computers, you can connect their parallel or serial ports using a special data transfer cable. For you to be able to create a network consisting of more than two computers, each computer needs a network card and special cables to connect the network cards to each other or to a central *hub*.

✅ Twisted-pair cables look like thick telephone cables. **BNC** cables look more like TV/VCR cables.

⚠️ **WARNING**
Shop carefully for network cards and make sure the ports on the card match the type of cabling you intend to use.

✅ To economically network two computers, you can connect them with a special data cable. Perform Tasks 2–6.

Task 1: Installing the Networking Hardware

Start Here

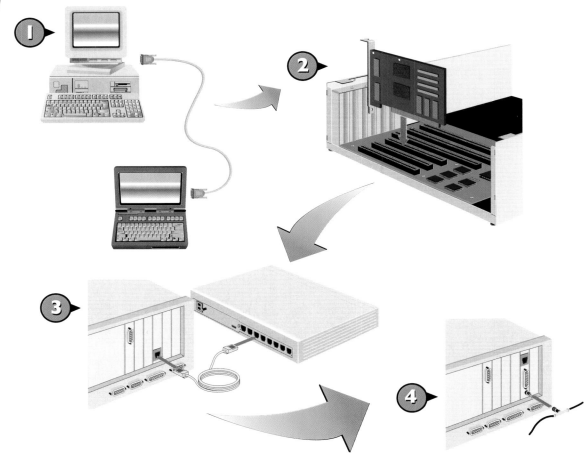

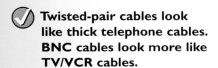

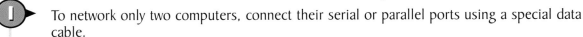

① To network only two computers, connect their serial or parallel ports using a special data cable.

② To network two or more computers, install a network card in each computer.

③ You can connect the network cards using twisted-pair cables that connect each computer to a central hub.

④ Alternatively, you can connect the network cards directly to each other using *BNC* cables.

Next Step

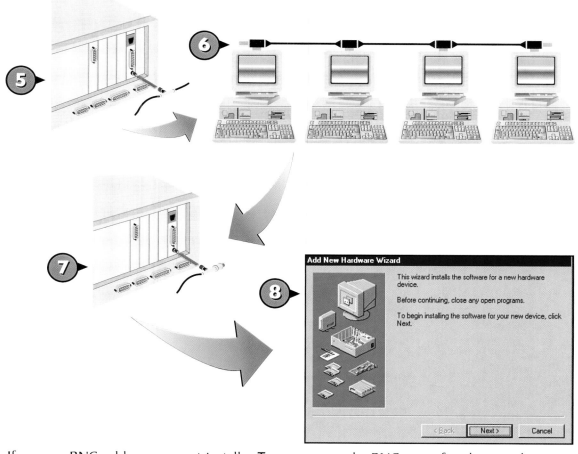

After you install your network cards and restart Windows, Windows should detect the card on each computer and lead you through the process of installing the required driver.

5 ▶ If you use BNC cables, you must install a *T-connector* on the BNC port of each network card.

6 ▶ Each computer on the network can be connected to two other computers using the T-connector.

7 ▶ If a computer is connected to only one other computer, cap the open leg of the T-connector with a *terminator*.

8 ▶ Restart the computers and use the Add New Hardware wizard to install the driver for each network card you installed.

Task 2: Installing the Windows Networking Components

Start Here

If you performed a standard Windows installation, the Windows networking components are not installed on your computer. In order to establish a connection between two or more computers, you must install these components on every computer you wish to network. This task leads you through the installation.

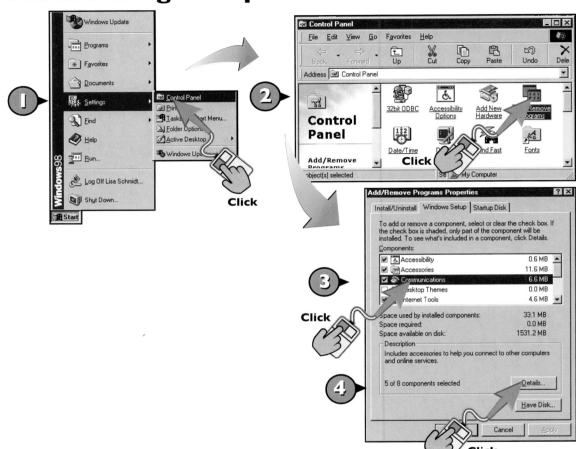

To network only two computers, you don't need to install network cards. You can connect the serial or parallel ports on two computers using a data cable.

1 ▶ Choose **Start**, **Settings**, **Control Panel**.

2 ▶ Click the **Add/Remove Programs** icon.

3 ▶ In the **Components** section of the **Windows Setup** tab, click **Communications**.

4 ▶ Click the **Details** button.

Next Step

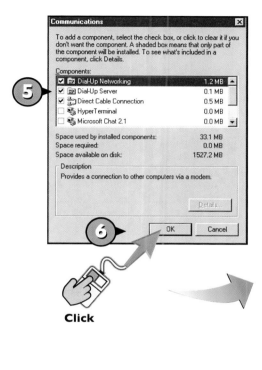

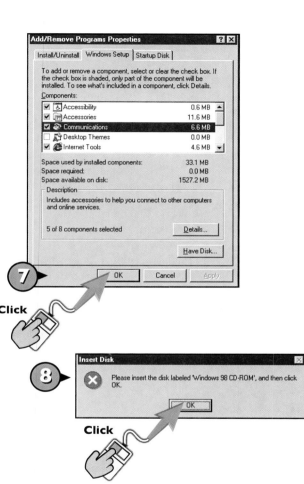

Windows installs three networking components: Dial-Up Networking for modem, Internet, and network support; Dial-Up Server, which allows you to connect from a remote location using a modem; and Direct Cable Connection, for connecting the serial or parallel ports on two computers using a special data cable.

Click

Click

Click

 Place a check mark next to **Dial-Up Networking**, **Dial-Up Server**, and **Direct Cable Connection**.

 Click **OK**.

 In the **Add/Remove Programs Properties** dialog box, click **OK** to save your changes.

 If prompted to insert the Windows 98 CD, insert the CD into your CD-ROM drive and click **OK**.

✓ **If you are setting up a network using network cards and cables, you need not install Dial-Up Server or Direct Cable Connection.**

Task 3: Adding Network Protocols

To communicate on a network, the networked computers must all speak the same language; that is, they must use the same *network protocol*. Windows supports three protocols: **TCP/IP** (for modem communications), **NetBEUI** (for fast data transfers), and **IPX/SPX** (for playing multi-player computer games over a network connection).

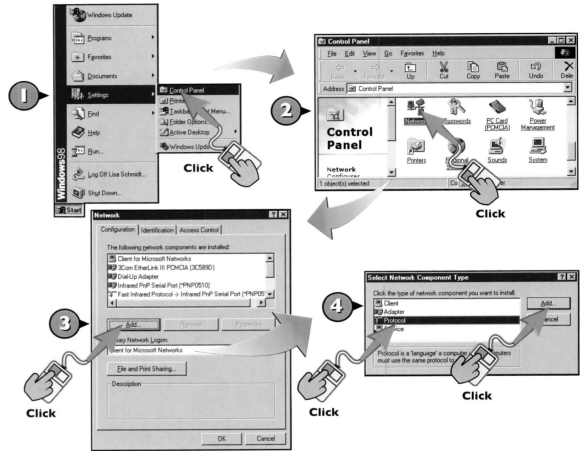

WARNING

If you have trouble connecting later, remove all but one of the protocols from all networked computers and try the connection again.

1 ▶ Choose **Start**, **Settings**, **Control Panel**.

2 ▶ Click the **Network** icon.

3 ▶ Click the **Add** button.

4 ▶ Click **Protocol** and click the **Add** button.

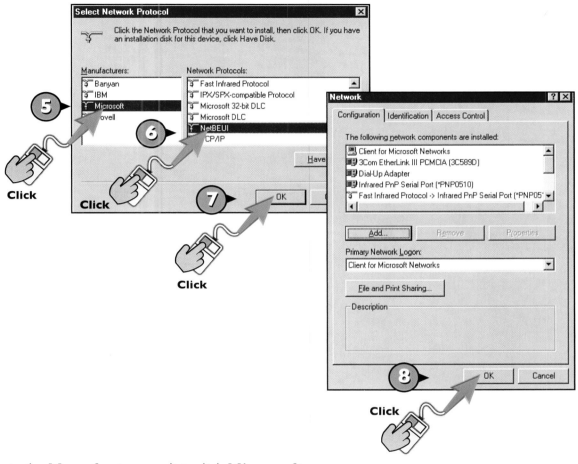

You must repeat these steps for every computer you plan to include in the network. Install the same protocol(s) on every computer.

5 ▶ In the **Manufacturers** list, click **Microsoft.**

6 ▶ Click **IPX/SPX-compatible Protocol**, **NetBEUI**, or **TCP/IP** to add a desired protocol.

7 ▶ Click **OK**.

8 ▶ When you return to the **Network** dialog box, click **OK** to save your changes and exit.

✔ To remove a protocol, display the **Network** dialog box, click the name of the protocol, and click **Remove.**

Task 4: Adding Client for Microsoft Networks

When two computers are networked, the computer that requests data acts as the *client*. The computer that fulfills the request is the *server*. On a peer-to-peer network, every computer plays both roles. In order for the computers to be able to interact, Client for Microsoft Networks must be installed on every computer.

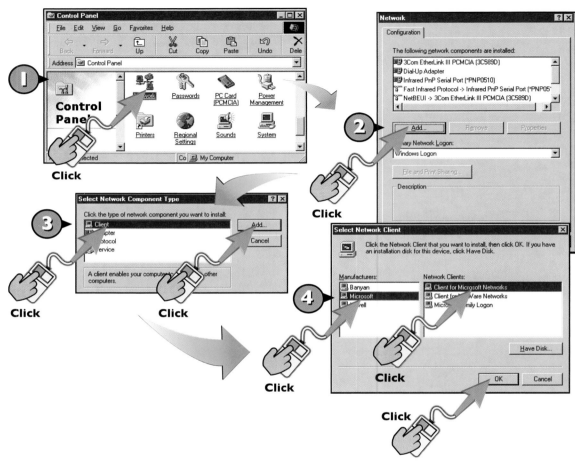

✓ If Client for Microsoft Networks is listed at the top of the **Network** dialog box, it is already installed.

① In the Control Panel, click the **Network** icon.

② Click the **Add** button.

③ Click **Client** and click **Add**.

④ Click **Microsoft** and click **Client for Microsoft Networks**. Click **OK**.

Task 5: Turning on File and Printer Sharing

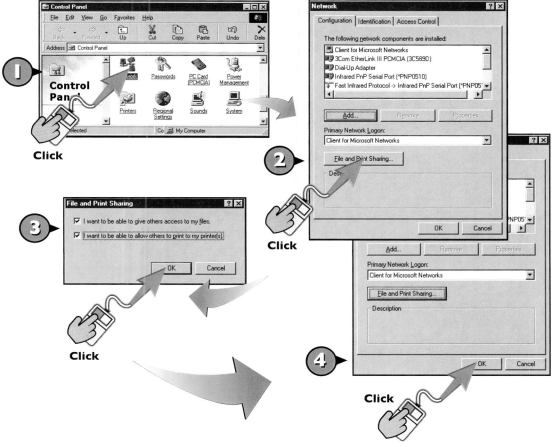

Click

Click

Click

Click

Before you can copy files from one computer to another or use another computer's resources on the network, that computer must give you permission. To set up a networked computer so other computers can access its resources, you must turn on file and printer sharing, as shown here.

① In the Control Panel, click the **Network** icon.

② Click the **File and Print Sharing** button.

③ Turn on the desired sharing option(s) and click **OK**.

④ Click **OK** to save your changes.

End Task

Task 6: Setting Up a Direct Cable Connection Between Two Computers

A direct cable connection is the most economical way to network two computers. Using a special data cable, you can connect the serial or parallel ports on two computers and then copy and paste files and folders between the two computers. (If you're setting up a bona-fide network, skip this task.)

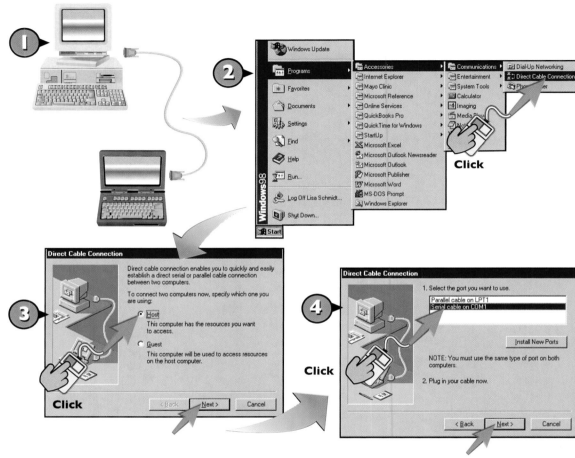

Click

Click

Click

✓ Connecting the parallel ports provides a faster connection, but you must disconnect the printer in order to use the ports.

1 Connect the serial or parallel ports on the two computers with your data cable, as explained in Task 1, "Installing the Networking Hardware."

2 On the host computer, choose **Start**, **Programs**, **Accessories**, **Communications**, **Direct Cable Connection**.

3 Click **Host** and click **Next**.

4 Select the port in which you plugged the data cable, click **Next**, and follow instructions until you see the **Finish** button.

Next
Step

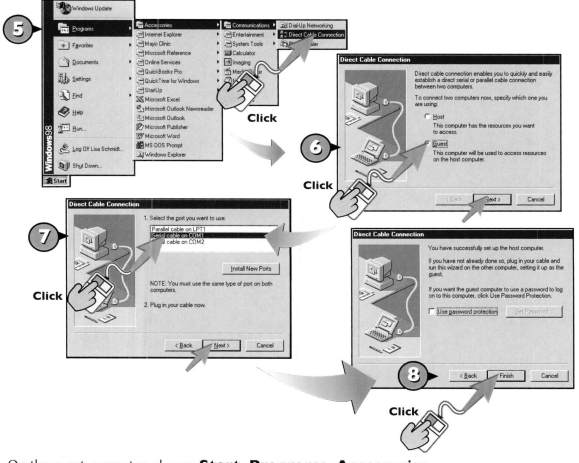

With a direct cable connection, one computer (usually the more powerful of the two) acts as the host and the other computer as the guest. The guest is typically the computer to which you are copying files, but you can copy and paste files in either direction.

5 On the guest computer, choose **Start**, **Programs**, **Accessories**, **Communications**, **Direct Cable Connection**.

6 Click **Guest** and click **Next**.

7 Select the port in which you plugged the data cable, click **Next**, and follow instructions until you see the **Finish** button.

8 Click **Finish** for the host computer, and then click **Finish** for the guest computer.

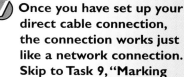
Once you have set up your direct cable connection, the connection works just like a network connection. Skip to Task 9, "Marking Network Resources as Shared," to learn how to share resources between the two computers.

End Task

Task 7: Entering Your Logon Preferences

Chances are that your computers are set up for logging on to Windows. In order to connect to the network, you must choose to log on to the network on startup. This task shows you what to do.

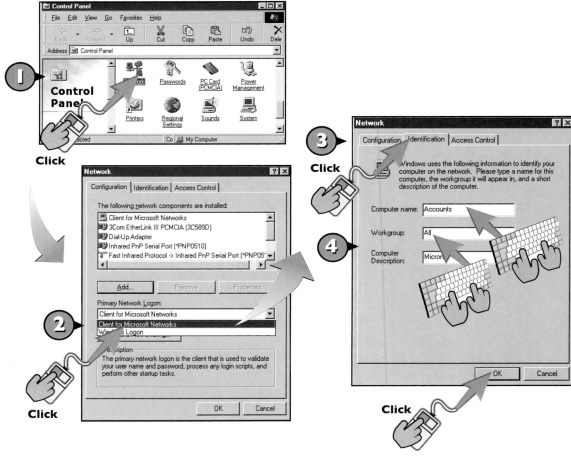

WARNING
You must enter the same workgroup name for each computer on the network. Otherwise, you won't be able to share resources.

Windows Logon logs you on to Windows 98 but does not display a warning if your computer fails to connect to the network on startup.

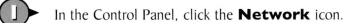

1 ▶ In the Control Panel, click the **Network** icon.

2 ▶ Open the **Primary Network Logon** drop-down list and choose **Client for Microsoft Networks**.

3 ▶ Click the **Identification** tab and enter a unique name for your computer in the **Computer name** text box.

4 ▶ Click in the **Workgroup** text box, and then type the name of the workgroup to which you belong. Click **OK**.

Task 8: Logging On and Off the Network

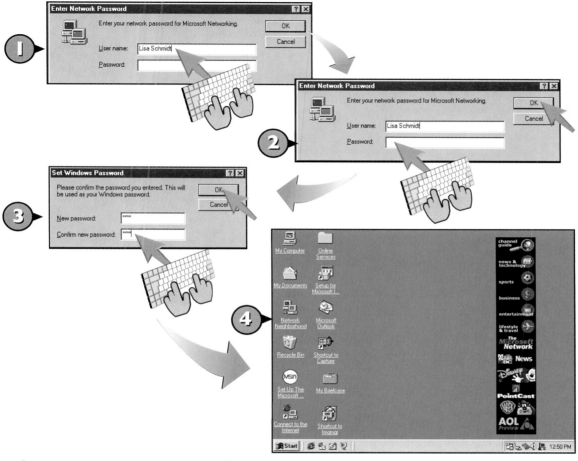

To connect your computer to the network, you must log on with your username and password. This identifies you on the network, and as a result, Windows establishes the connection between your computer and the other computers on the network so you can access shared files and resources.

 When you start your computer, Windows displays the **Enter Network Password** dialog box. Type your name in the **User name** box.

 In the **Password** text box, type a password (or leave it blank to log on without a password). Click **OK**.

 If you entered a password, you are prompted to confirm. Type the password and click **OK**. (This dialog box appears only the first time you log on.)

 You are logged on to Windows and the network, even though nothing looks any different, yet.

 Windows should prompt you to enter your logon name at startup. If you don't see the prompt, choose **Start, Logoff**.

Before you can access disks, folders, files, and printers on your network, the person whose resources you want to use must give you access to the computer's resources. By default, Windows allows you to turn on sharing for specific disks, folders, files, and printers, as shown here.

Task 9: Marking Network Resources as Shared

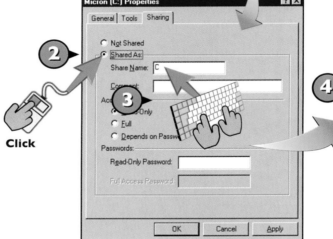

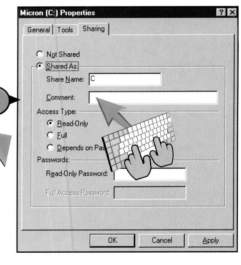

You can change the access type to **User-Level** in the **Network** dialog box to share by user instead of by resource.

 In My Computer, right-click the icon for the disk or folder you want to share and click **Sharing**.

 Click **Shared As**.

 If you wish, change the name of the resource in the **Share Name** text box.

 If you wish, type any additional information in the **Comment** text box.

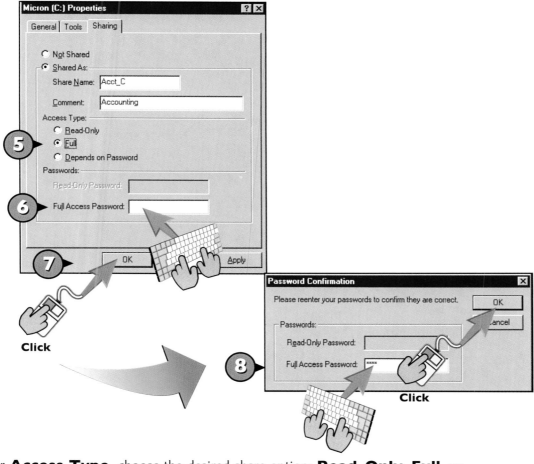

When you mark a resource as shared, a hand appears below the resource's icon, indicating that it is a shared resource.

Click

Click

Page
151

5 Under **Access Type**, choose the desired share option: **Read-Only**, **Full**, or **Depends on Password**.

6 Under **Passwords**, type the password that people must enter in order to access the shared resource (this step is optional).

7 Click **OK**.

8 If you entered a password, Windows prompts you to confirm it. Type the password again and click **OK**.

These steps show how to mark disks, folders, and files as shared. To share a printer, right-click its icon, choose **Sharing**, enter your preferences, and click **OK**.

End Task

Once resources are marked as shared, you can access those resources from other computers on the network using the Windows Network Neighborhood, as shown here.

Task 10: Accessing Shared Resources with Network Neighborhood

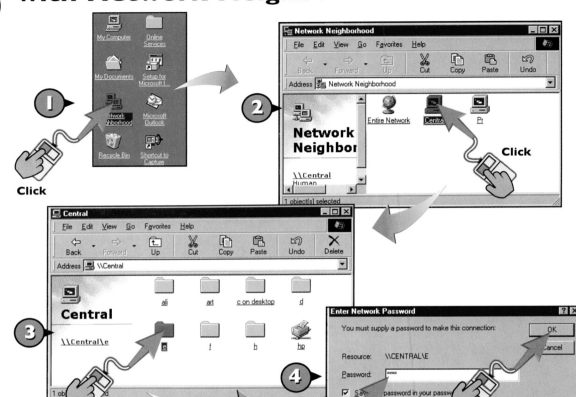

1 Click the **Network Neighborhood** icon on the Windows desktop.

2 Click the icon for the computer you want to access.

3 Click the icon for the drive or folder you want to access. (Drive icons are displayed as folders.)

4 If accessing the resource requires a password, enter the required password and click **OK**.

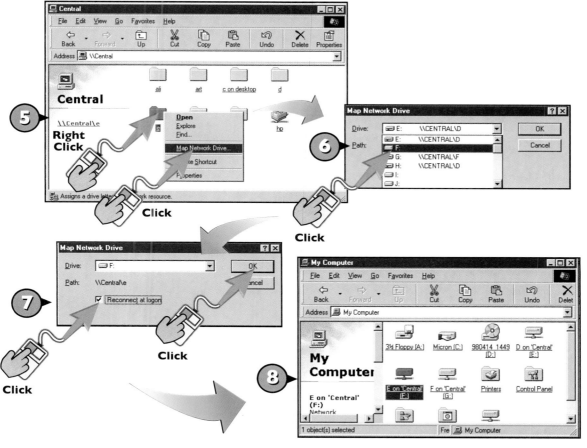

For easier access to disks and folders on the network computer, you can *map* a disk or folder to your computer. You can then use folders and files just as if they were on your computer; you can access them using **File, Save As** or **File, Open** in your applications.

5 In Network Neighborhood, right-click the disk or folder that you want to map to your computer and choose **Map Network Drive**.

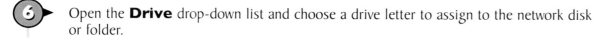

6 Open the **Drive** drop-down list and choose a drive letter to assign to the network disk or folder.

7 To have Windows automatically log on to this disk or folder on startup, click **Reconnect at logon**. Click **OK**.

8 In My Computer, an icon for the disk or folder appears, just as if the disk or folder were installed on your computer.

Task 11: Using a Network Printer

Using a printer over a network connection is a two-step process. You must first mark the printer as shared (as shown in the previous task) and then install the printer on the computer from which you want to print. These steps show you how to install the shared printer.

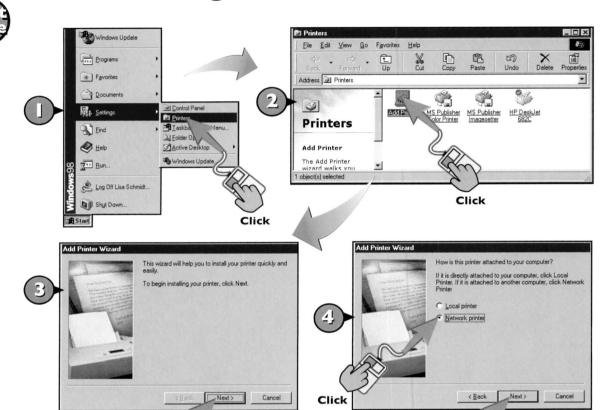

1. ▶ Choose **Start**, **Settings**, **Printers**.

2. ▶ Click the **Add Printer** icon.

3. ▶ When the **Add Printer Wizard** dialog box appears, click **Next**.

4. ▶ Choose **Network printer** and click **Next**.

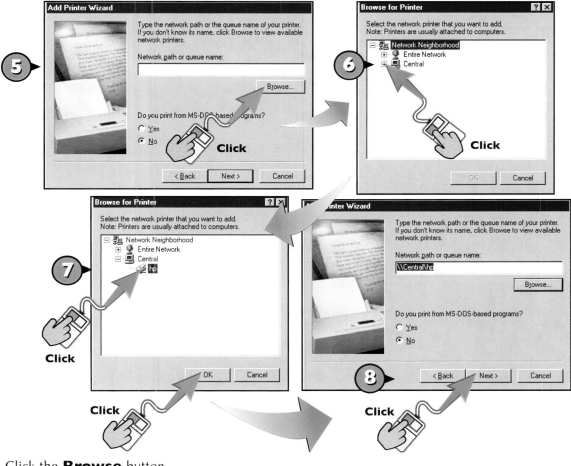

When you install a network printer, Windows copies the printer driver from the computer connected to the printer to your computer, so you can use the printer just as if it were connected to your computer.

 Click the **Browse** button.

 Click the plus sign next to the computer to which the printer is connected.

 Click the printer's icon and click **OK**.

 Click **Next** and follow the wizard's instructions to complete the installation.

⚠ WARNING
You can print files as you normally do. However, make sure the printer is on and is loaded with paper before you start printing.

Task 12: Sending Messages Across the Network

If you work on a network, you can use a utility called *WinPopup* to send messages to your colleagues on the network and to read messages sent by others. This task shows you how to set up and use WinPopup.

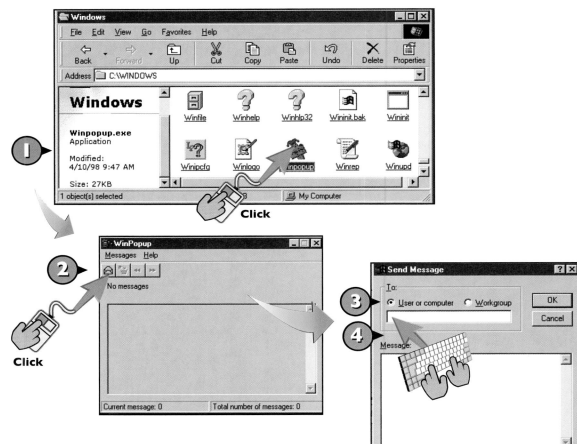

Start Here

Click

Click

WARNING
If WinPopup is not installed, use Add/Remove Programs (from the Control Panel) to install it.

1 ▶ In My Computer, navigate to the **Windows** folder and click **WinPopup**. Repeat this step on all of the networked computers.

2 ▶ To send a message, click the **Send** button.

3 ▶ Click **User or computer** (to send a message to an individual) or **Workgroup** (to send a message to everyone in the workgroup).

4 ▶ Type the name of the user, computer, or workgroup in the **To** text box.

Next Step

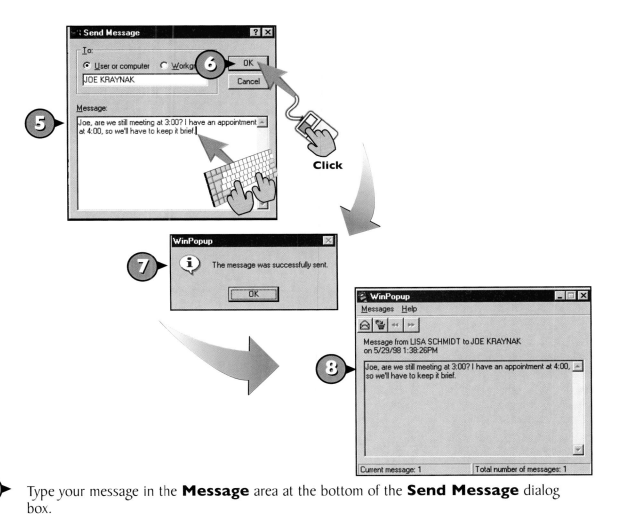

Click

5 Type your message in the **Message** area at the bottom of the **Send Message** dialog box.

6 Click **OK**.

7 WinPopup notifies you as to whether the message was properly transmitted.

8 The message pops up on the screens of those people to whom you addressed the message.

✓ To ensure that everyone on the network is running WinPopup, add it to the **Windows Startup** menu on each computer. You can drag the **WinPopup** icon from the **Windows** folder over **Start, Programs, Startup,** and then drop it on the **Startup** menu.

✓ To configure WinPopup, open the **Messages** menu, select **Options,** and enter your preferences.

Task 13: Setting Up Your Own Intranet

Although standard networks are still popular, more and more companies are restructuring their networks to look and act like the Internet. This new type of network is called an *intranet* (an internal Internet). This task shows you how to set up Personal Web Server on your network to make your own mini intranet.

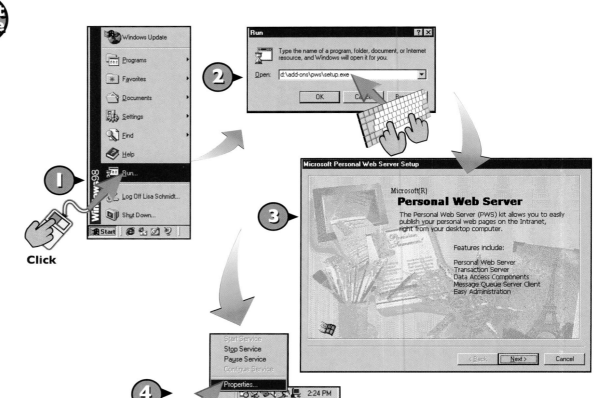

1 ▶ Insert the Windows 98 CD into your CD-ROM drive, and then open the **Start** menu and choose **Run**.

2 ▶ Type **d:\add-ons\pws\setup.exe** (where **d** is the letter of your CD-ROM drive) and press **Enter**.

3 ▶ Follow the onscreen instructions to install Personal Web Server. Restart Windows when prompted.

4 ▶ Right-click the **Personal Web Server** icon in the system tray and choose **Properties**.

Next Step

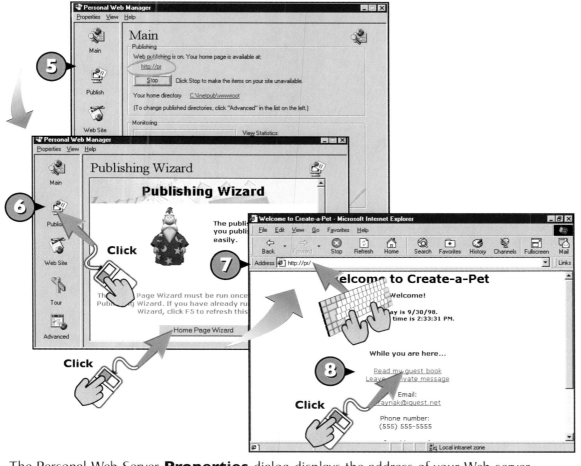

Once Personal Web Server is installed, you can place Web pages on the server and then open them just as if they were on the Web. The Personal Web Server **Properties** window contains the tools you need to immediately create a custom page and place it on your Web server.

5 The Personal Web Server **Properties** dialog displays the address of your Web server. Write it down.

6 Click the **Publish** icon, click **Home Page Wizard**, and follow the wizard's instructions to create and publish a custom home page.

7 To access the Web server, run Internet Explorer and enter the Web server's address (for example, **http://pr/**).

8 You can click links to skip from one Web page or document to another, just as you navigate the Web.

 Personal Web Server is a pretty complex tool. To learn more about how to use it, check out its help system.

Windows 98 Tips, Tricks, and Shortcuts

Windows 98 is faster and more reliable than its predecessor, but you'll still be twiddling your thumbs during startup and while Windows is performing any complex task. Fortunately, you can improve the performance of Windows and learn some tricks to help yourself work more efficiently.

This part contains a collection of Windows performance enhancements and timesaving tips, along with illustrated instructions that show you how to take advantage of advanced Windows 98 Web features.

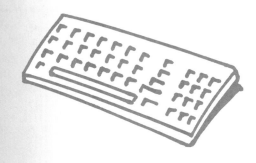

Tasks

Task 1: Making Windows Start Faster

Windows 98 doesn't like to get out of bed in the morning. On startup, you watch the opening screen and listen to your hard drive crank away, wondering if Windows will ever get around to displaying the desktop. One technique for making Windows start faster is to prevent programs from running on startup, as shown here.

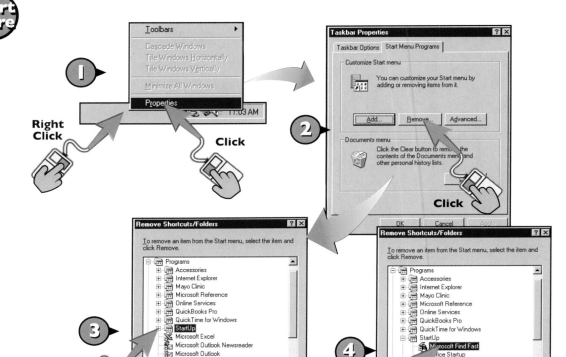

⊘ WARNING

If you have an anti-virus program that runs on startup, don't remove it from the **StartUp** folder.

⊘ To have Windows restart more quickly, click the **Start** button, choose **Shut Down**, click **Restart**, and then hold down the **Shift** key while clicking the **OK** button.

1 ▸ Right-click a blank area of the taskbar and click **Properties**.

2 ▸ Click the **Remove** button in the **Start Menu Programs** tab.

3 ▸ Click the plus sign next to the **StartUp** folder.

4 ▸ Click the name of a program you don't want Windows to run on startup and click **Remove**.

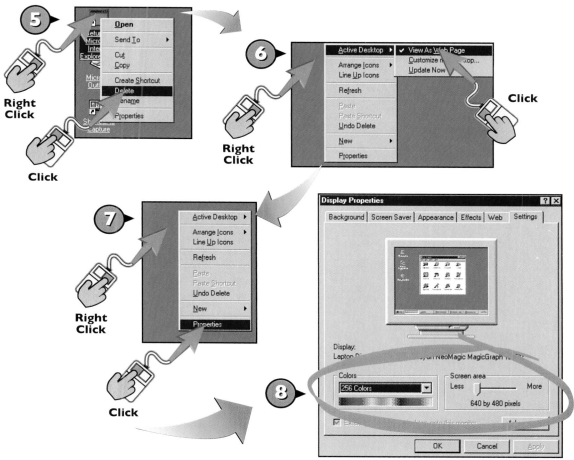

Although desktop shortcuts are timesavers, they take time to display on startup; if you don't use a shortcut, you should delete it, as shown here. Also, the Windows Web page desktop takes extra time to load on startup; consider turning off the View As Web Page option.

⑤ To delete a shortcut, right-click the shortcut icon and click **Delete**.

⑥ To turn off **View As Web Page**, right-click a blank area of the desktop, point to **Active Desktop**, and click **View As Web Page**.

⑦ Right-click a blank area of the desktop and click **Properties**.

⑧ On the **Settings** tab, set the number of screen colors to **256** and decrease the screen resolution to **800 by 600** or **640 by 480**.

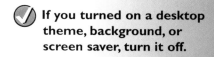
If you turned on a desktop theme, background, or screen saver, turn it off.

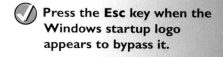
Press the **Esc** key when the Windows startup logo appears to bypass it.

End Task

Task Scheduler is a new Windows tool that allows you to set up programs to run and automatically perform specific tasks—such as scanning your hard drive for errors or backing up files—at a specified date and time. These steps show you how to schedule a task.

Task 2: Scheduling Tasks to Run Automatically

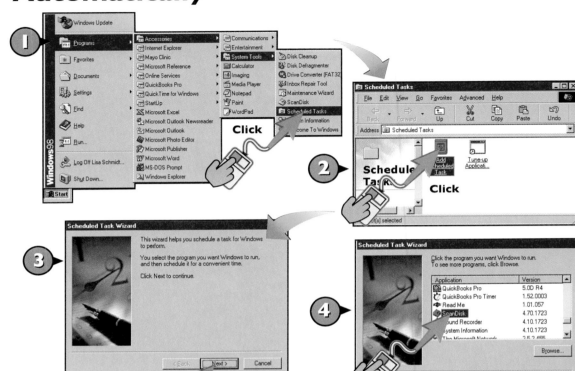

1 ▶ Click **Start**, **Programs**, **Accessories**, **System Tools**, **Scheduled Tasks**.

2 ▶ Click the **Add Scheduled Task** icon.

3 ▶ When the Scheduled Task wizard appears, click the **Next** button.

4 ▶ Click the program that you want Task Scheduler to run automatically, and click **Next**.

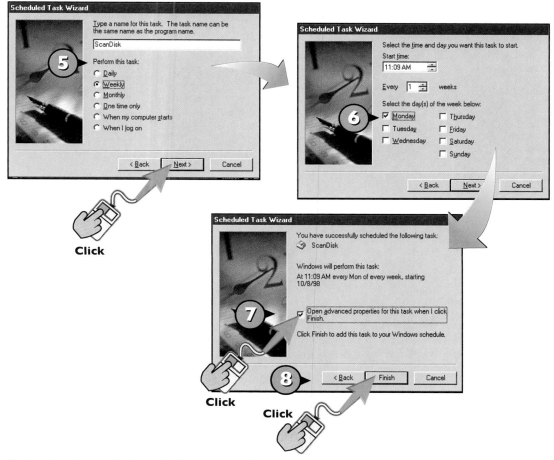

After you set up a program to run automatically, Windows runs Task Scheduler on startup, which launches the program at the scheduled time. The Task Scheduler icon appears in the system tray (right end of the taskbar); right-click it to display a menu for opening or pausing Task Scheduler.

Click

Click

Click

⑤ Select the desired schedule for running the program and click **Next**.

⑥ Specify the time and days you want the program to run and click **Next**.

⑦ (Optional) Click **Open advanced properties...** so you can enter specific settings for this program.

⑧ Click the **Finish** button.

⚠ **WARNING**
Many of the options available in Task Scheduler vary depending on the program you choose to run.

✔ To disable Task Scheduler, double-click its icon in the system tray, open Task Scheduler's **Advanced** menu, and click **Stop Using Task Scheduler**.

Task 3: Saving Time with Your Keyboard

Windows was built for mice, designed to make it easy for users to enter commands by pointing and clicking. However, you can work more efficiently in Windows by learning a few common keystrokes.

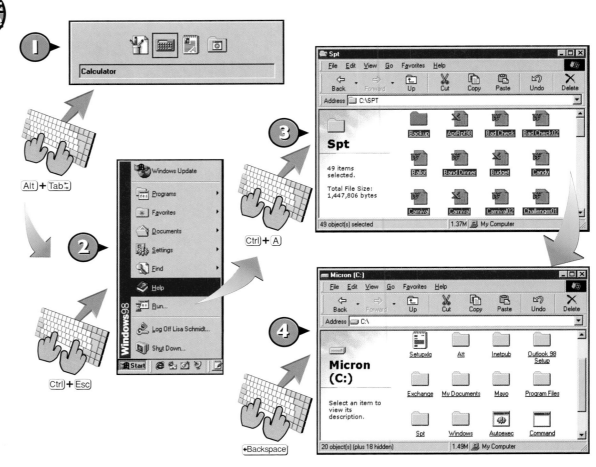

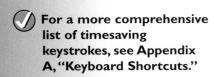 For a more comprehensive list of timesaving keystrokes, see Appendix A, "Keyboard Shortcuts."

 Hold down the **Alt** key while pressing the **Tab** key to choose a currently running application, and then release both keys.

 Press **Ctrl+Esc** to open the **Start** menu, use the arrow keys to highlight the desired option, and press **Enter**.

 In My Computer, Windows Explorer, and most Windows applications, you can press **Ctrl+A** to select everything.

 In My Computer or Windows Explorer, press **Backspace** to move up one level in the folder list.

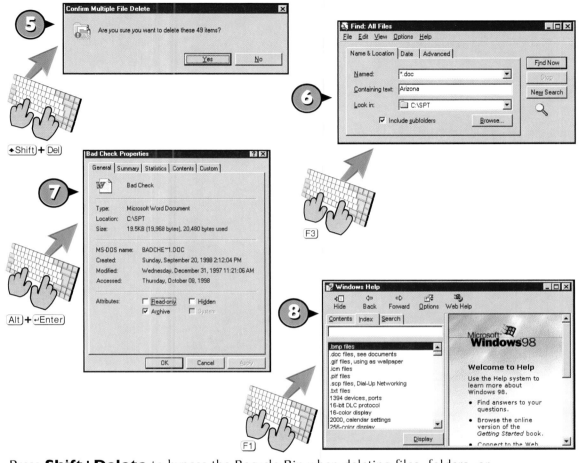

Page
167

5 ▶ Press **Shift+Delete** to bypass the Recycle Bin when deleting files, folders, or shortcuts. (Be careful.)

6 ▶ Press **F3** to open the **Find: All Files** dialog box, so you can search for a file by name or contents.

7 ▶ Press **Alt+Enter** to view the properties of the currently selected object.

8 ▶ Press **F1** to get help.

WARNING
Some keystrokes, such as F1 and F3, will not work in Windows if a currently active application uses the same keystroke. If you have problems using a particular keystroke, minimize your application windows.

Task 4 : Streamlining Operations with Your Mouse

You have mastered the basic mouse moves: pointing, clicking, and dragging. However, Windows includes a few hidden mouse moves that can help you streamline the most time-consuming tasks. This task shows you the most helpful mouse moves.

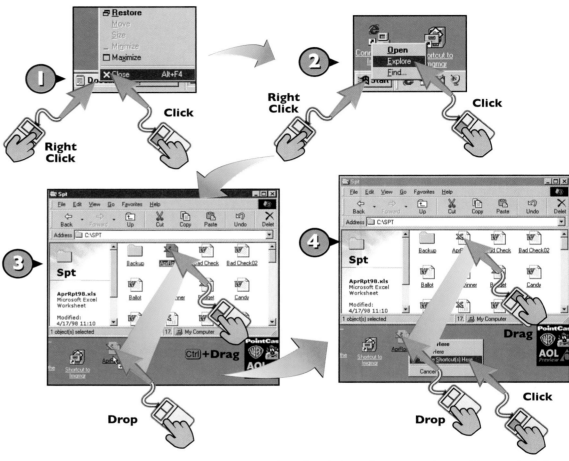

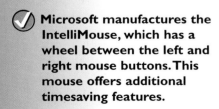

Microsoft manufactures the IntelliMouse, which has a wheel between the left and right mouse buttons. This mouse offers additional timesaving features.

 To exit a program whose window is minimized, right-click its button in the taskbar and click **Close**.

 Right-click the **Start** button and click **Explore** to display the **Start Menu** folder and its subfolders in Windows Explorer.

 To quickly copy a file, hold down the **Ctrl** key while dragging it from one folder to another or to the Windows desktop.

 To quickly create a shortcut, right-drag the icon to the desired location, drop it, and click **Create Shortcut(s) Here**.

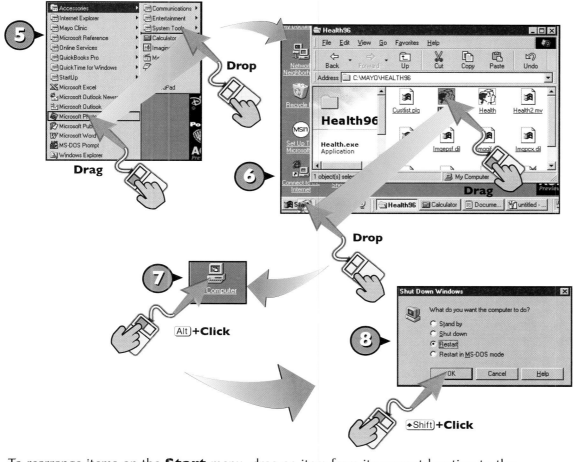

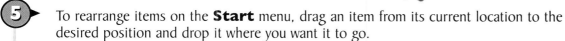

5 To rearrange items on the **Start** menu, drag an item from its current location to the desired position and drop it where you want it to go.

6 To place a program, folder, or file at the top of the **Start** menu, drag its icon over the **Start** button and drop it.

7 **Alt+click** an item to display its properties.

8 When restarting windows, **Shift+click** the **OK** button to prevent Windows from reloading all the startup commands.

Task 5: Saving Time with Shortcuts

Although desktop shortcuts slow down the Windows startup, they can save you time as you work. You can place shortcuts on the desktop for disks or folders you frequently open, the programs you use most often, and even documents that you often refer to or edit.

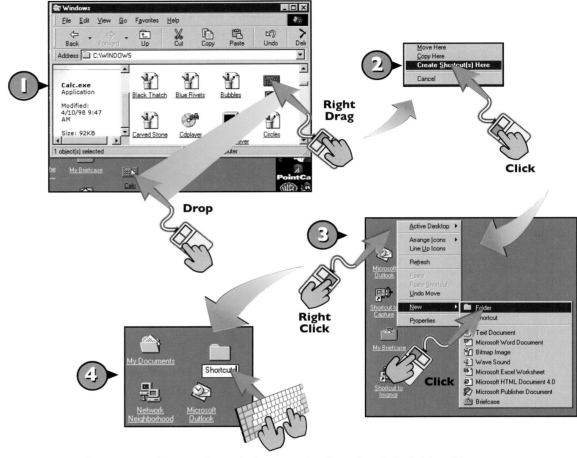

Start Here

Right Drag

Drop

Right Click

Click

Click

✓ To reduce the number of shortcuts on the Windows desktop, create a folder on the desktop and place new shortcuts in that folder.

1 To create a shortcut on the Windows desktop, right-drag the disk, folder, file, or program icon to the desktop.

2 Release the mouse button and click **Create Shortcut(s) Here**.

3 To create a folder for your shortcuts, right-click the desktop and choose **New**, **Folder**.

4 Type a name for the folder and press **Enter**.

Next Step

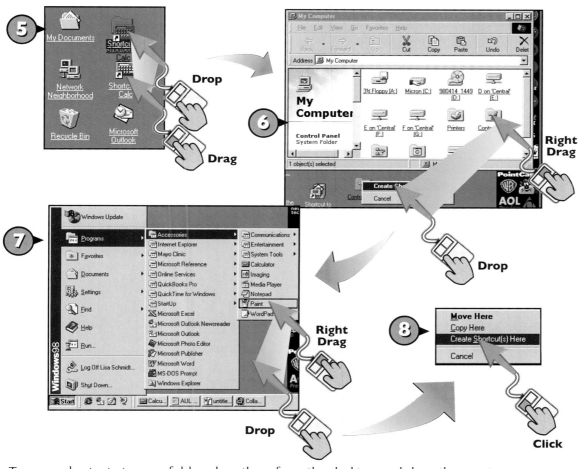

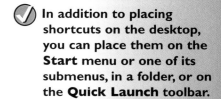

5 ► To move shortcuts to your folder, drag them from the desktop and drop them onto your new folder icon.

6 ► For convenient access to the Windows Control Panel, place a shortcut for the Control Panel on the desktop.

7 ► Right-drag any submenu or program from the **Start** menu or one of its submenus to the Windows desktop.

8 ► Click **Create Shortcut(s) Here**.

✓ **In addition to placing shortcuts on the desktop, you can place them on the Start menu or one of its submenus, in a folder, or on the Quick Launch toolbar.**

The taskbar offers a fairly quick way to change from one program to another by clicking buttons. You can also use **Alt+Tab**, as explained in Task 3, "Saving Time with Your Keyboard," to switch programs. Another way to quickly run or switch to a specific program is to assign it a unique shortcut key, as shown here.

Task 6: Switching Programs with a Keystroke

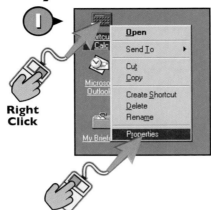

Start Here

Right Click

Click

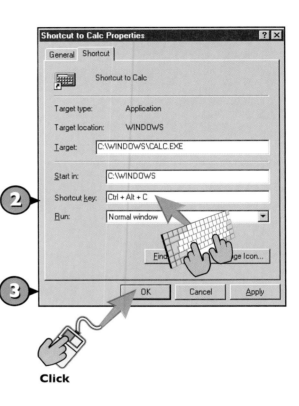

Shortcut to Calc Properties

General | Shortcut

Shortcut to Calc

Target type: Application

Target location: WINDOWS

Target: C:\WINDOWS\CALC.EXE

Start in: C:\WINDOWS

Shortcut key: Ctrl + Alt + C

Run: Normal window

OK | Cancel | Apply

Click

✓ **To quickly run or switch to the program, hold down Ctrl+Alt while pressing the key you assigned to the program.**

1 ▶ Right-click the icon or shortcut you use to run the program and click **Properties**.

2 ▶ In the **Shortcut key** text box, hold down the **Ctrl** key while pressing the desired letter, number, or symbol key.

3 ▶ Click **OK**.

End Task

Task 7: Opening and Printing Documents with Drag and Drop

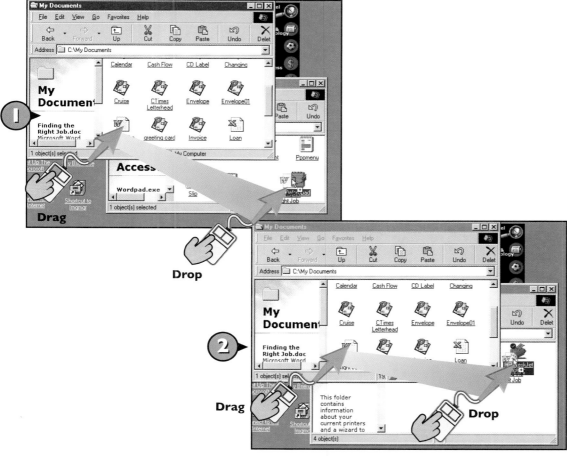

You've used the drag-and-drop technique to copy and move files and folders, but you can also use it to open and print documents, as shown here.

Drag

Drop

Drag

Drop

 Display the icon for the document file you want to open and the icon for the program you want to use. Drag the document file icon and drop it on the program icon.

 To print a file, display the icon for the document file you want to print and the icon for your printer. Drag the document file icon and drop it on the printer icon.

 A faster way to open a document file is to click its icon. When you install a program, Windows sets up a file association between the program and the file types it can open.

Task 8: Right-Click Printing

Printing with drag and drop requires that you display the document icon and the printer icon on screen at the same time, which may take a little juggling. A faster way to print is to use a context menu, as shown here.

 In My Computer, select the document file(s) you want to print.

 Right-click one of the document files and click **Print**.

Task 9: Copying Data Between Documents with Scraps

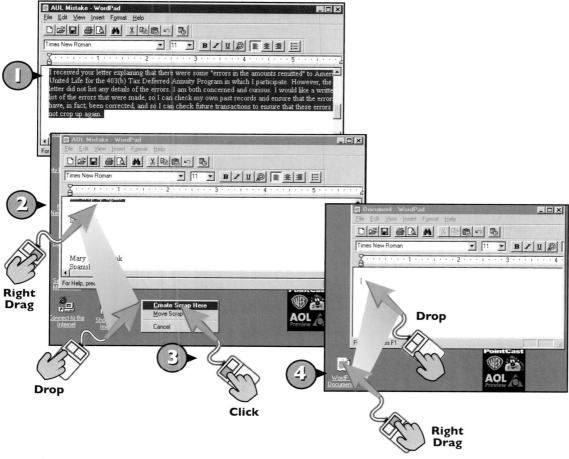

Right Drag

Drop

Click

Drop

Right Drag

Desktop shortcuts typically represent programs or entire document files. However, you can create shortcuts that contain selected text from one of your documents. These shortcuts, called *scraps*, let you quickly insert the text in other documents.

 Open the document that contains the text or other data you want to use as a scrap and select the data.

 Right-drag the selection and drop it on the Windows desktop.

 Click **Create Scrap Here**.

 You can right-drag the scrap into another document to insert the copied data.

 Create a scrap for data you commonly use, such as your mailing address.

Task 10: Copying Files to a Floppy Disk with Send To

In Windows Explorer, you can quickly copy files from one disk to another by dragging selected files from the file list and dropping them onto a disk icon in the folder list. In My Computer, you need to display two windows or use the **Send To** command, as shown here.

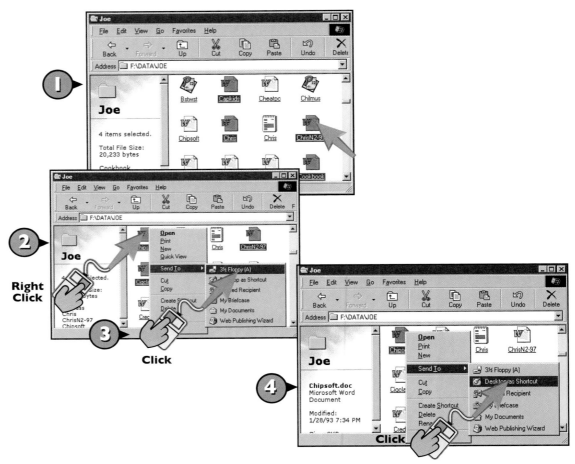

Right Click

Click

Click

✓ Right-click the **Start** button and choose **Explore.** Click the **Send To** folder. You can add shortcuts for disks and folders to this menu to have them listed on the Send To menu.

1. In My Computer, select the file(s) you want to copy to the floppy disk.

2. Right-click one of the selected files.

3. Point to **Send To**, and click the drive that contains the disk.

4. You can also use **Send To** to quickly create shortcuts on the Windows desktop.

Task 11: Placing the Recent (Documents) Folder on Your Desktop

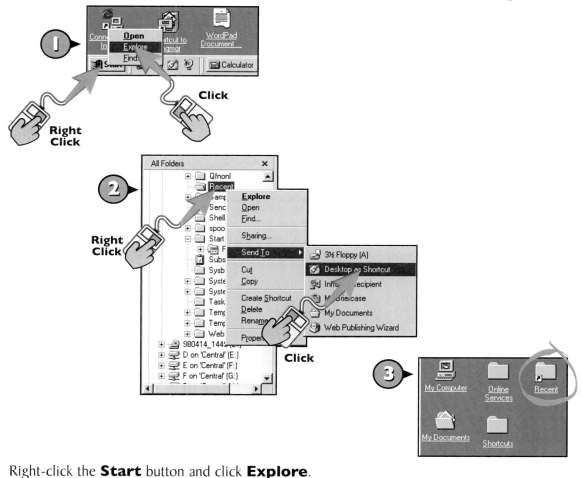

Right Click

Click

Right Click

Click

You may already know that Windows keeps track of the 15 most recently opened documents on the **Start, Documents** menu. You can quickly open documents by choosing them from the **Documents** menu, so you don't have to hunt them down. To make the **Documents** menu more easily accessible, add a shortcut to it on the desktop.

1. Right-click the **Start** button and click **Explore**.

2. Right-click the **Recent** folder in the folder list, point to **Send To**, and click **Desktop as Shortcut**.

3. Return to the desktop to see your new shortcut.

✓ If the **Recent** folder is not displayed, choose **View, Folder Options**, click the **View** tab, and turn on **Show All Files.**

Task 12: Muting Your Modem

Your modem might just be the loudest, most annoying device connected to your computer. If the sounds that your modem emits bother you, you can mute the modem, disabling its speaker.

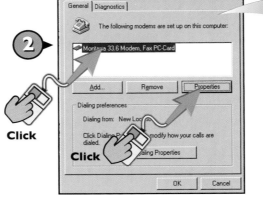

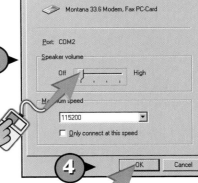

Click

Click

Click

Click & Drag

Click

If the **Speaker Volume** slider is grayed, click the **Connection** tab, click the **Advanced** button, type atm0 (zero, not O) in the **Extra Settings** text box, and click **OK**.

1 In the Windows Control Panel, click the **Modems** icon.

2 Click the modem you want to mute and click **Properties**.

3 Drag the **Speaker volume** slider all the way to the left.

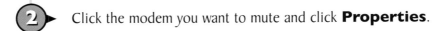

4 Click **OK**.

Task 13: Ejecting CDs from Windows

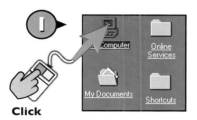

Click

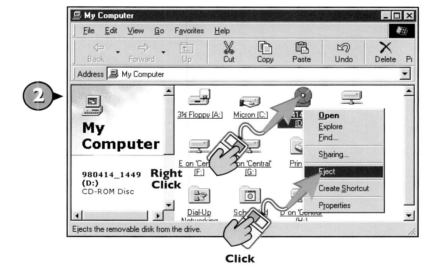

Click

You can save **wear-and-tear** on your **CD-ROM** drive's Eject button by ejecting the disk from **Windows. This** also allows you to quickly eject the disk without having to reach over to the **CD-ROM** drive.

1 ▶ Click **My Computer**.

2 ▶ Right-click the icon for your CD-ROM drive and choose **Eject**.

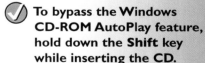 To bypass the Windows **CD-ROM** AutoPlay feature, hold down the **Shift** key while inserting the **CD**.

In many cases, you may want to refer to a document without actually opening it or preview a document to determine if it's the one you want to open. You can do this with Quick View, as shown here.

Task 14: Previewing Documents with Quick View

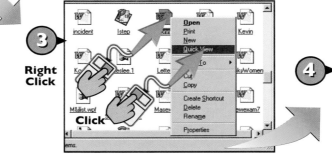

Right Click

Click

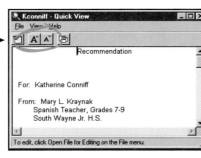

 To preview a graphic file, point to it in My Computer.

 My Computer displays a thumbnail version of the image in the left pane, assuming **View As Web Page** is on.

 To preview a document, right-click the document file and click **Quick View**.

 If desired, click the **Increase Font Size** or the **Decrease Font Size** button to change the displayed text size.

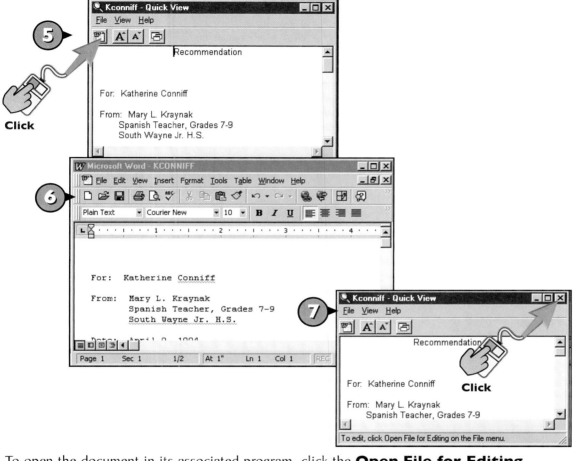

Quick View allows you to preview both document (text) files and graphic (picture) files. However, Quick View may not have the viewer required for displaying all file types. If you right-click a file and the Quick View command is not listed, the viewer is not available.

⑤ To open the document in its associated program, click the **Open File for Editing** button.

⑥ Quick View opens the program associated with this document file type, and the program opens the document.

⑦ To close the Quick View window, click its **Close** button.

✓ **To view a graphic file, right-click its icon in My Computer or Windows Explorer and click Preview.**

End Task

Page
181

Task 15: Making a Simple Web Page

Windows 98 includes a program, called *FrontPage Express,* for creating and editing Web pages. FrontPage Express features a Web Page wizard that can lead you step-by-step through the process of creating a simple Web page.

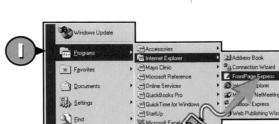

If you find a Web page you like, open it in FrontPage Express and modify it to make it your own. However, you should obtain permission from the creator of the original page.

 To run FrontPage Express, click **Start**, **Programs**, **Internet Explorer**, **FrontPage Express**.

 Open the **File** menu and click **New**.

 Click **Personal Home Page Wizard** and click **OK**.

 Place a check mark next to each section you want to include (you can edit the sections later). Click **Next**.

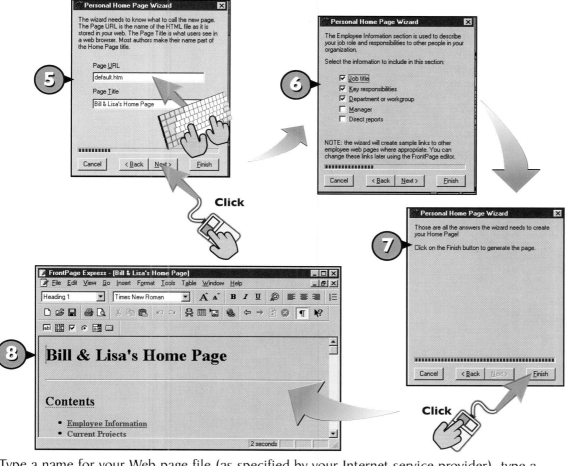

Click

Click

The Personal Home Page wizard asks a series of questions and prompts you to enter text that you want to include on your Web page. These steps vary depending on the choices you made in step 4.

5 ▶ Type a name for your Web page file (as specified by your Internet service provider), type a page title, and click **Next**.

6 ▶ Follow the wizard's instructions to enter additional information you want to include on your page.

7 ▶ After you answer all of the wizard's questions, click the **Finish** button.

8 ▶ The wizard creates your page and displays it in FrontPage Express.

 Store your Web page and all graphic files and other associated files in a single folder to make it easier to transfer the page to the Web later.

 End Task

Task 16: Adding Links

Without links that point to other Web pages, your Web page is a dead end that people won't choose to revisit. You can easily transform existing text or images into links that point to Web pages at your site or at other sites on the Web.

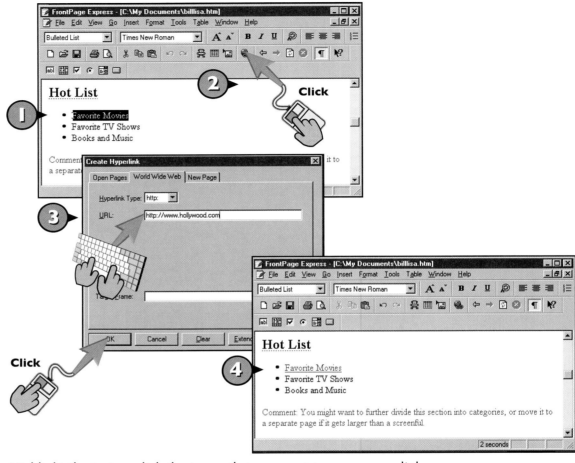

✔ Drag links and images from pages displayed in Internet Explorer and drop them onto your Web page displayed in FrontPage Express.

 Highlight the text or click the image that you want to use as your link.

 Click the **Create or Edit Hyperlink** button.

 Type **http://** followed by the page address you want the link to point to and click **OK**.

 If you used text as the link, it appears blue and underlined.

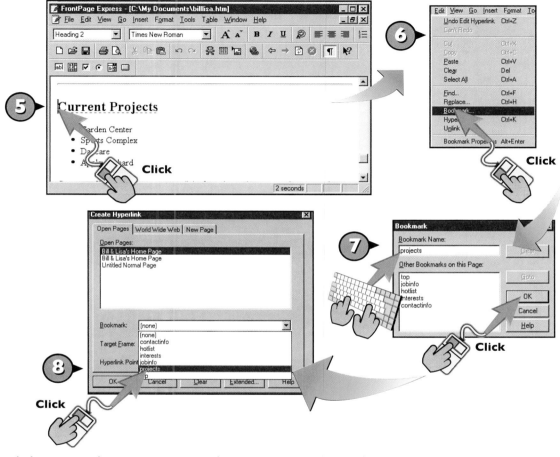

If you have a long Web page, insert an outline of the page at the top and then transform the items in the outline into links that point to different areas on your page. You do this by inserting bookmarks at the destination points and then inserting links that point to the bookmarks.

5 Click to move the insertion point where you want to insert the target.

6 Open the **Edit** menu and click **Bookmark**.

7 Type a name for the bookmark and click **OK**.

8 Create a link, but choose the name of the target or bookmark instead of entering a page address.

⚠ **WARNING**
It's illegal to use original text or graphics without written permission from the author or artist.

FrontPage Express allows you to post your page to the Web using the **File, Save** command. This runs the Web Publishing wizard, which leads you step-by-step through the process of transferring your page and all associated files to a Web or FTP server.

Task 17: Publishing Your Web Page

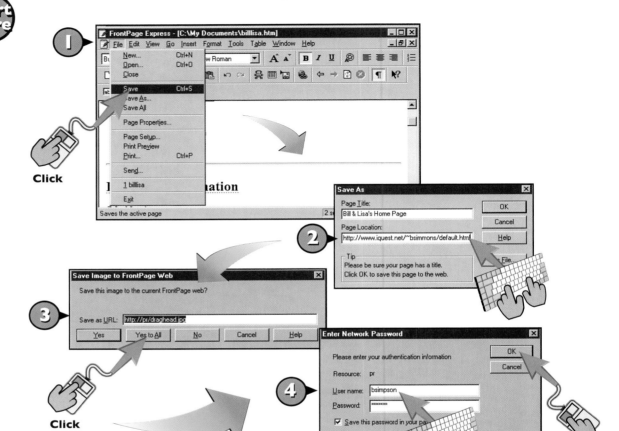

Start Here

Click

Click

Click

Click

WARNING

Obtain the Web or FTP server address from your Internet service provider along with instructions on how to log on to the server and the name of the directory in which you should place your file(s).

1 ▶ Open the **File** menu and select **Save**.

2 ▶ In the **Page Location** box, type the address where you need to post your page, followed by its filename. Click **OK**.

3 ▶ If the wizard asks whether you want to save an associated file to the server, click **Yes to All**.

4 ▶ Enter your username and password and click **OK**.

Next Step

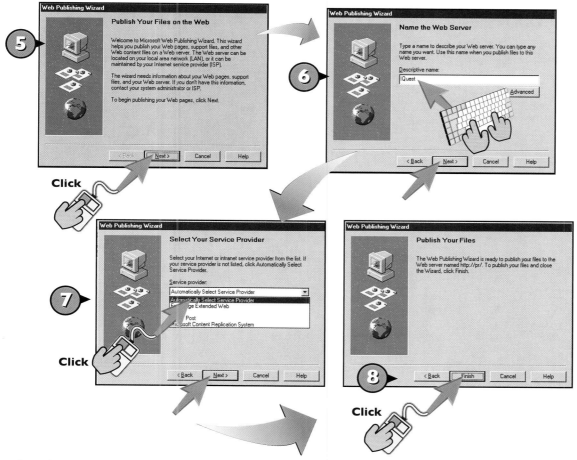

Click

Click

Click

When the Web Publishing wizard displays its introduction, click **Next**.

Type a name for the Web server and click **Next**.

When prompted to select the service provider type, choose **Automatically Select Service Provider**. Click **Next**.

Follow the wizard's instructions and then click the **Finish** button to start transferring your Web page(s).

✓ To quickly publish pages, select the Web page file and associated files in My Computer. Right-click one of the files, point to **Send To**, and click **Web Publishing Wizard**.

WARNING
The steps you take for publishing your files may vary depending on how your Internet service provider manages files.

End Task

Task 18: Using a Graphic as the My Computer Background

When you turn on **View As Web Page**, My Computer uses a Web page as the background, displaying the bar on the left that shows information about the selected object. You can use a graphic image as the background, if desired. For example, you might want to use your company logo as the background.

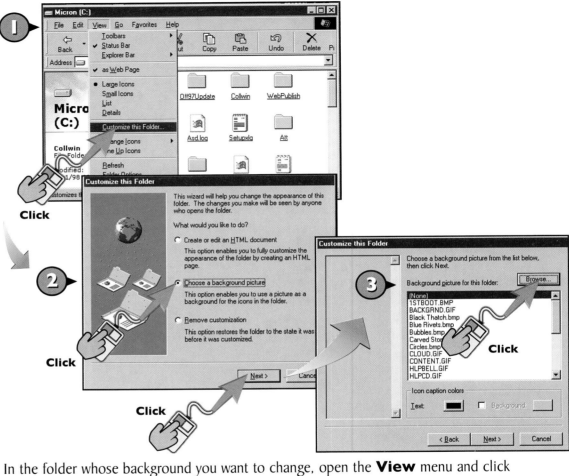

Click

Click

Click

Click

✓ You can customize the Web page background that Windows uses, but the procedure is complicated and requires a thorough knowledge of HTML (Web) codes.

1 ▸ In the folder whose background you want to change, open the **View** menu and click **Customize this Folder**.

2 ▸ Click **Choose a background picture** and click **Next**.

3 ▸ Click the **Browse** button.

Next Step

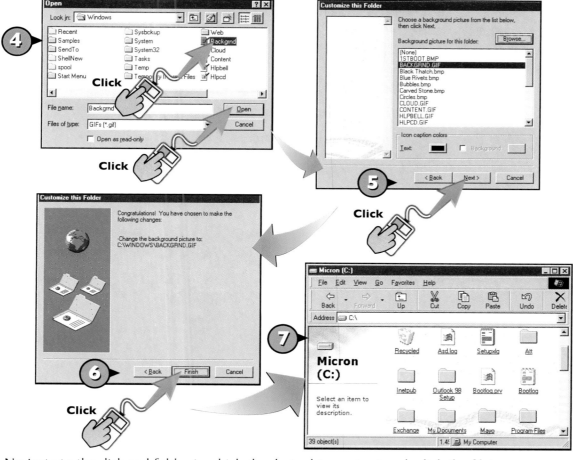

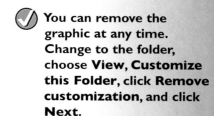

4 Navigate to the disk and folder in which the desired image is stored, click the file's name, and click **Open**.

5 Click **Next**.

6 Click **Finish**.

7 The new graphic background appears in My Computer, but only for this folder.

You can remove the graphic at any time. Change to the folder, choose **View, Customize this Folder, click Remove customization,** and click **Next**.

To make all your folders use this same background, choose **View, Folder Options,** click the **View** tab, and click **Like Current Folder**.

Troubleshooting
Windows 98

Microsoft claims that Windows 98 is more reliable, and more crash resistant, than Windows 95. However, it's still not crash proof. Your hardware drivers (the programs that tell Windows how to communicate with installed devices) and applications may have bugs that cause problems for which Windows cannot be held responsible.

When things don't go just right, the tasks in this section can help. Here, you will learn how to recover when your system locks up, safely restart your computer, find and install the latest hardware drivers, resolve device conflicts, and use many of the new Windows system utilities to help you track down and correct problems on your own.

Tasks

Task 1: Recovering When Windows Locks Up

Occasionally, when you're working in your application, Windows will stop responding. You may not be able to click an option or even move the mouse. Before doing anything, wait a couple minutes to see if Windows will snap out of it. If Windows remains locked up, take these steps to recover.

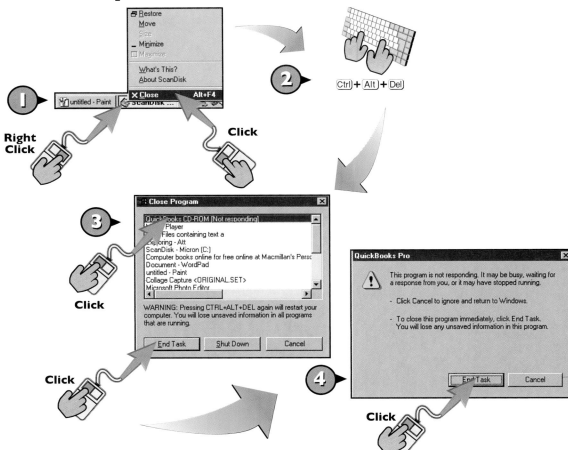

Right Click

Click

Click

Click

Click

Click

Start Here

⚠ WARNING
If possible, save your work and close any programs before performing these steps to prevent data loss.

✓ Make a Windows Startup disk for emergencies. In the **Add/Remove Programs** dialog box, click the **Startup Disk** tab, click the **Create Disk** button, and follow instructions.

1 ▶ Use the taskbar to switch to any currently running programs and close them.

2 ▶ If your system is still locked up, press **Ctrl+Alt+Delete**.

3 ▶ Click the program that has **[Not responding]** next to its name and click the **End Task** button.

4 ▶ Click **End Task** again.

Next Step

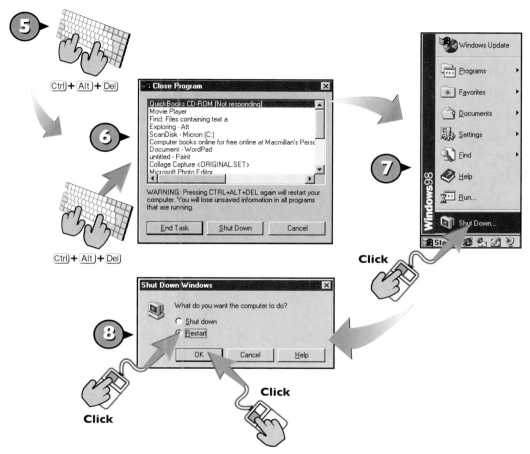

5 ▸ If your system still does not respond, press **Ctrl+Alt+Del**.

6 ▸ Press **Ctrl+Alt+Delete** when the **Close Program** dialog box appears.

7 ▸ In some cases, Windows may restart in Safe Mode. If it does, open the **Start** menu and click **Shut Down**.

8 ▸ Click **Restart** and click **OK**.

Windows 98 comes with several troubleshooters that can help you determine the causes of common hardware problems and help you correct them. Troubleshooters help by displaying a series of questions that lead you through checks and corrections. This task shows you what to expect.

Task 2: Using the Windows Troubleshooters

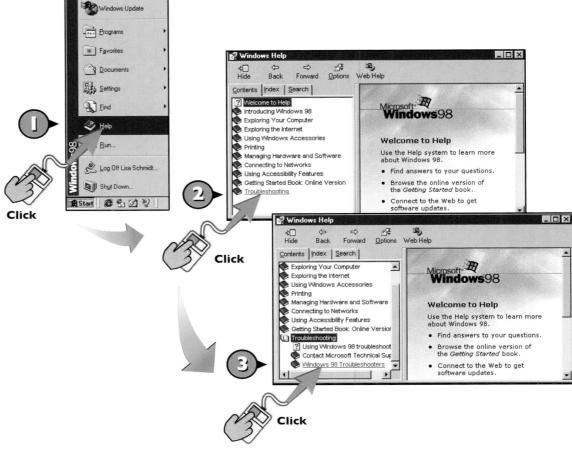

Click the **Start** button and click **Help**.

In the **Contents** list, click **Troubleshooting**.

Click **Windows 98 Troubleshooters**.

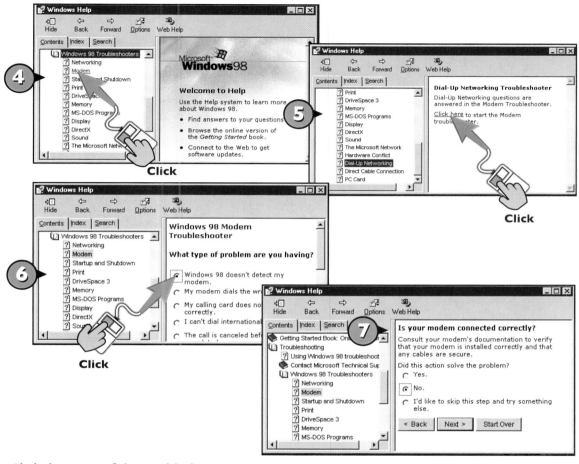

4 ▸ Click the name of the troubleshooter you want to use.

5 ▸ If the troubleshooter doesn't run automatically, click the button or link for running the troubleshooter.

6 ▸ Click the problem you're experiencing and press **Enter**.

7 ▸ Follow the troubleshooter's instructions

If the troubleshooters can't solve the problem, you may need track down the conflict and tinker with some hardware settings on your own. To determine hardware conflicts, you use the Windows Device Manager.

Task 3: Tracking Down Hardware Conflicts

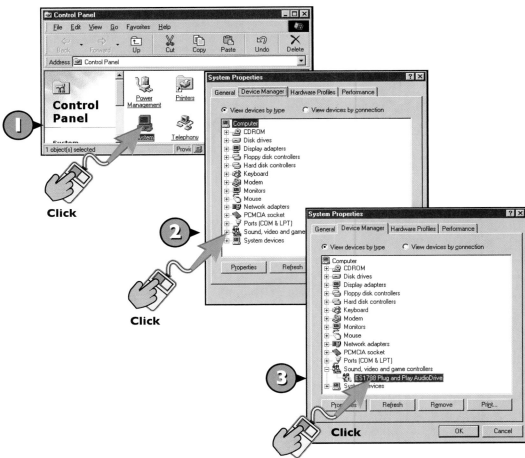

To quickly access the **System Properties** dialog box without opening the Control Panel, Alt+click **My Computer.**

1. Open the Windows Control Panel and click the **System** icon.

2. In the **Device Manager** tab of the **System Properties** dialog box, click the plus sign next to the type of device that's having problems.

3. If a yellow caution icon appears next to the name of the device, there is a conflict. Click the device.

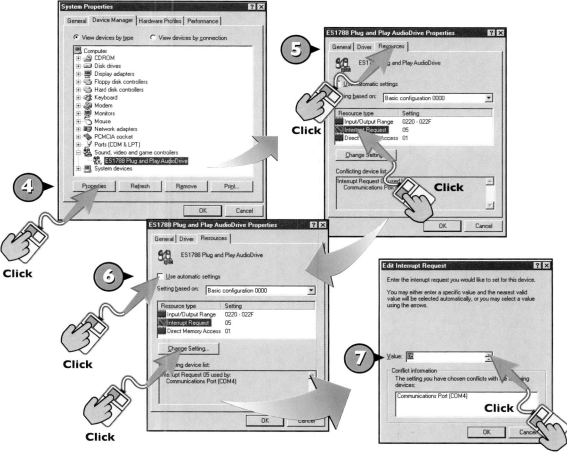

Most new devices are plug-and-play compatible, allowing Windows to determine the best settings for the device. However, if a device does not support plug and play, you may have to use jumpers or switches on the device to change the interrupt request, input/output range, or direct memory access channel.

---

④ ▶ Click the **Properties** button.

⑤ ▶ Click the **Resources** tab to display the conflict information, and click the conflicting setting.

⑥ ▶ To change a setting, remove the check mark next to **Use automatic settings** and click the **Change Setting** button.

⑦ ▶ Click the up or down arrow next to the **Value** text box to choose a setting that does not conflict with another device and click **OK**.

✅ Keep a written log of any changes you make to your system, so you can return to the original settings.

End Task

Task 4: Installing Updated Device Drivers

Every device requires a *device driver* that tells Windows how to communicate with the device. Hardware manufacturers frequently update device drivers to correct problems and enhance performance. If you have problems with a device, installing the updated driver may help.

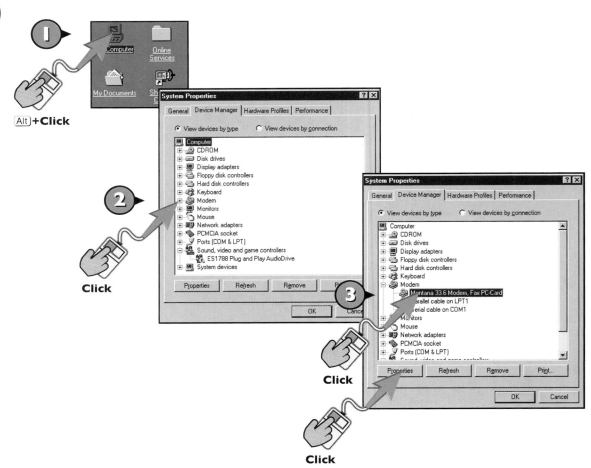

Alt+**Click**

Click

Click

Click

 Hardware manufacturers commonly post updated drivers on their Web sites. Check the documentation for the address of the manufacturer's Web site.

 Alt+click the **My Computer** icon.

 In the **Device Manager** tab, click the plus sign next to the type of device whose driver you want to update.

 Click the name of the device and click the **Properties** button.

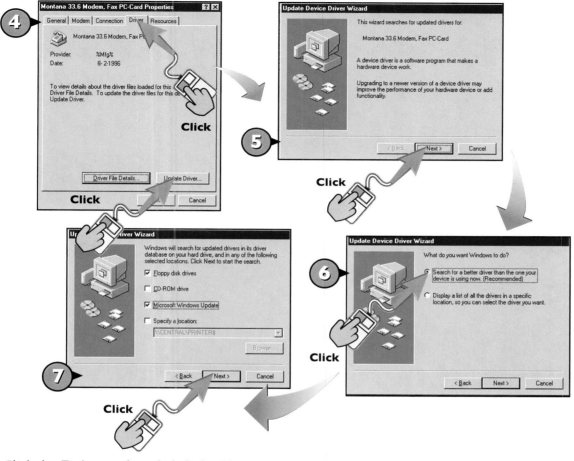

These steps show you how to use the **Update Device Driver** wizard to search for and install an updated driver. You must tell the wizard where to look: floppy disk drive, CD-ROM drive, Microsoft Windows Update (Microsoft's Web site), or a specific folder on your hard disk (if you copied the driver from the manufacturer's Web site).

④ Click the **Driver** tab and click the **Update Driver** button.

⑤ In the **Update Device Driver Wizard** dialog box, click the **Next** button.

⑥ Make sure **Search for a better driver...** is selected and click the **Next** button.

⑦ Choose the locations you want Windows to search for a driver, click **Next**, and follow the onscreen instructions.

 If you choose Microsoft Windows Update, you will have to register your copy of Windows 98 online.

End Task

Task 5: Getting Your Modem to Work

Windows may have trouble determining the type of modem installed on your computer and figuring out which communications port it should use. If you install a modem and have trouble using it or your mouse after the installation, you'll need to check the modem's settings.

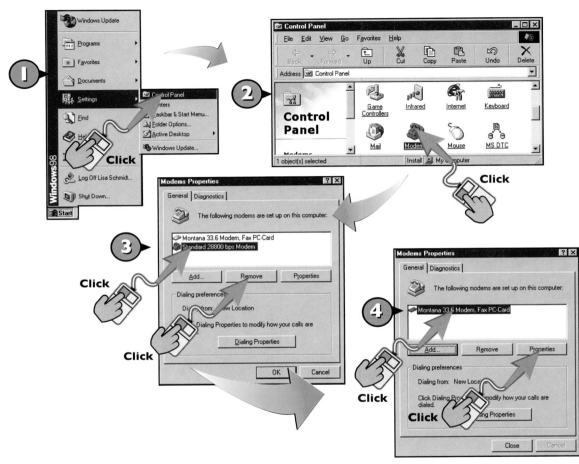

✓ Communications ports (COM ports) 1 and 3 commonly conflict, as do COM ports 2 and 4. If your mouse uses COM1, try setting your modem to use COM2 or COM4.

1 ▶ Click **Start**, **Settings**, **Control Panel**.

2 ▶ In the Control Panel, click the **Modems** icon.

3 ▶ If you have only one modem installed, but two are listed, click the name of the modem you don't use and click **Remove**.

4 ▶ Click the name of your modem and click the **Properties** button.

Next Step ▶

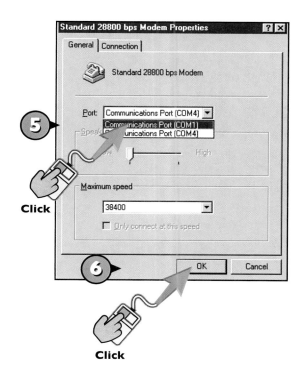

Click

Click

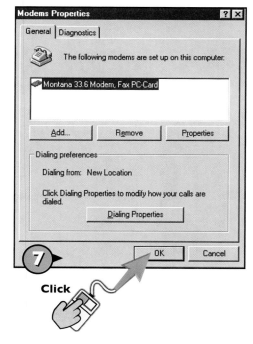

Click

If changing **COM** ports does not resolve the problem, check for device conflicts, as shown in Task 3, "Tracking Down Hardware Conflicts." When checking for conflicts on the **Device Manager** tab, focus on the **Modem, Mouse,** and **Ports** groups.

5 Open the **Port** drop-down list and choose a port that is not used by another device, such as your mouse.

6 Click **OK** to return to the **Modems Properties** dialog box.

7 Click the **OK** button to save your settings and exit.

If your mouse plugs into a PS/2 port (a round port like your printer uses), the modem typically uses COM1. If your modem connects to a serial port, the modem typically uses COM2.

End Task

Task 6: Troubleshooting Audio Problems

Audio problems are tough to track down, because so many variables are at work. The sound card might conflict with another device, speaker volume may be set too low, your microphone may not be working, or your CD-ROM driver may be causing problems. Take these steps to correct common problems.

✓ If your sound card has a volume control, crank it up and check the volume control(s) on your speakers. Also, make sure the speakers are connected to the output jacks; it's easy to confuse the jacks.

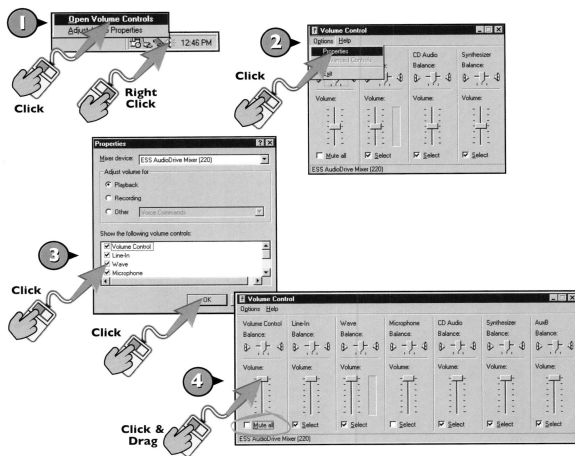

1 ▶ Right-click the **Volume** icon in the system tray and choose **Open Volume Controls.**

2 ▶ Open the **Options** menu and click **Properties**.

3 ▶ Place a check mark next to all of the volume controls in the list except **PC Speaker**, and click **OK**.

4 ▶ Make sure **Mute all** is off, drag all volume sliders up, and then click the **Close** button.

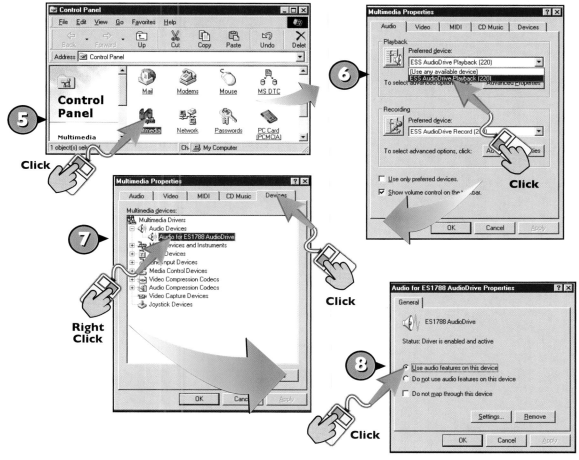

If you insert a music CD and it doesn't start playing, click **Start**, **Programs**, **Accessories**, **Entertainment**, **CD Player**, and click the **Play** button.

If your computer still has trouble playing sounds, run the Sound Troubleshooter, as shown in Task 2, "Using the Windows Troubleshooters."

5 ▶ Open the Windows Control Panel and click the **Multimedia** icon.

6 ▶ On the **Audio** tab, under **Playback**, open the **Preferred device** drop-down list and choose your sound card.

7 ▶ On the **Devices** tab, click the plus sign next to **Audio Devices**, right-click your sound card, and click **Properties**.

8 ▶ Make sure **Use audio features on this device** is selected. Click **OK** two times.

Task 7: Calibrating Your Joystick

Installing a joystick is fairly easy. You plug it into the game port and use the **Add New Hardware** wizard to install the joystick driver. However, making your joystick behave requires that you calibrate it, as shown here.

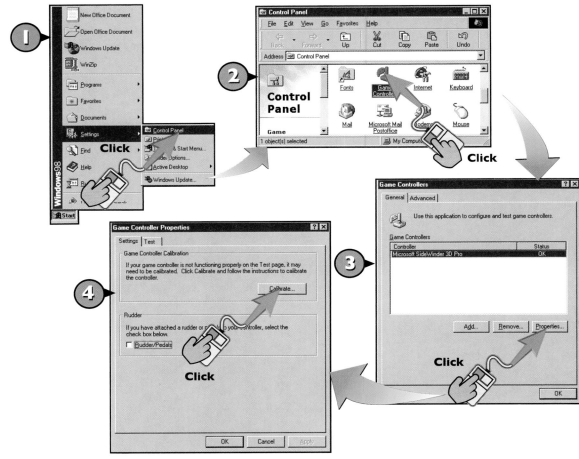

 Click **Start**, **Settings**, **Control Panel**.

 Click the **Game Controllers** icon.

 Click the joystick you want to calibrate and click the **Properties** button.

 Click the **Calibrate** button.

Next Step

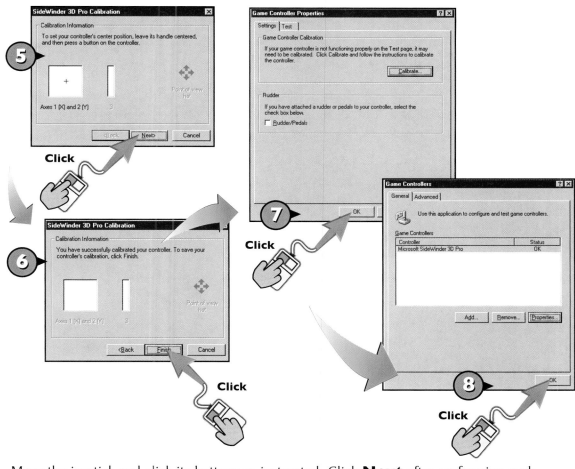

5 Move the joystick and click its buttons as instructed. Click **Next** after performing each step in the calibration.

6 When you are done, Windows displays a message indicating that the calibration has been successfully completed. Click **Finish**.

7 Click **OK** to return to the **Game Controllers** dialog box.

8 Click **OK** to save your changes.

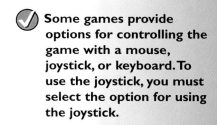 Some games provide options for controlling the game with a mouse, joystick, or keyboard. To use the joystick, you must select the option for using the joystick.

 End Task

Task 8: Solving Mouse Problems

If you can move the mouse pointer, but the mouse pointer is jumpy, clean the mouse ball and gently pick the dust off the rollers inside the mouse. If no mouse pointer is visible onscreen, fixing the problem in Windows is tough, because you need to navigate with the keyboard, as shown here.

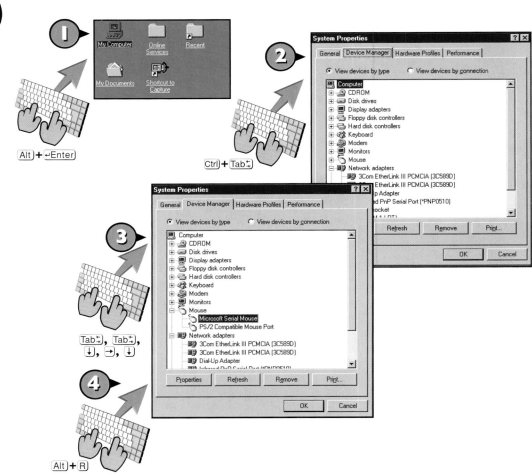

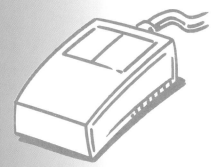

① ▶ Use the arrow keys to highlight the **My Computer** icon, and press **Alt+Enter**.

② ▶ Press **Ctrl+Tab** to change to the **Device Manager** tab.

③ ▶ Press **Tab** twice, press **down arrow** to highlight **Mouse**, press **right arrow**, and press **down arrow** to highlight your mouse.

④ ▶ Press **Alt+R** to choose **Properties**.

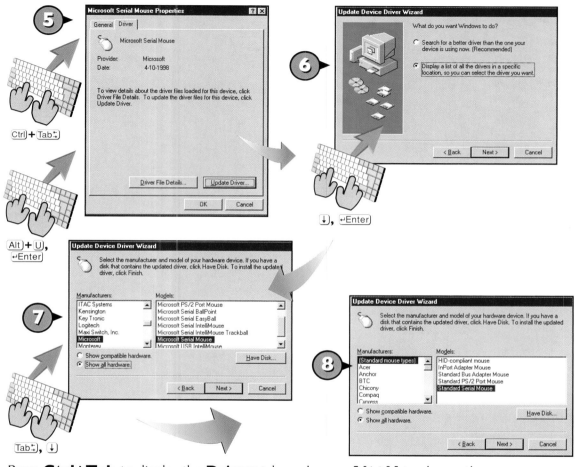

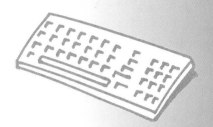

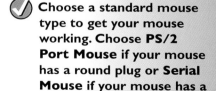

5 ▸ Press **Ctrl+Tab** to display the **Driver** tab, and press **Alt+U** to change the mouse driver. Press **Enter**.

6 ▸ Press **down arrow** to choose **Display a list of all the drivers...** and press **Enter**.

7 ▸ Press **Tab** and then **down arrow** to choose **Show all hardware**.

8 ▸ Use the **Tab** and arrow keys to choose a standard mouse type. Use the keyboard to save your settings, exit, and restart Windows. (See Part 7, Task 3.)

✓ **Choose a standard mouse type to get your mouse working. Choose PS/2 Port Mouse if your mouse has a round plug or Serial Mouse if your mouse has a rectangular plug.**

Task 9: Correcting Display Problems

If your display is grainy, too big, or too small, or if Windows starts in Safe Mode, you should check your display adapter and monitor settings. These steps show you how to check the settings and make some adjustments.

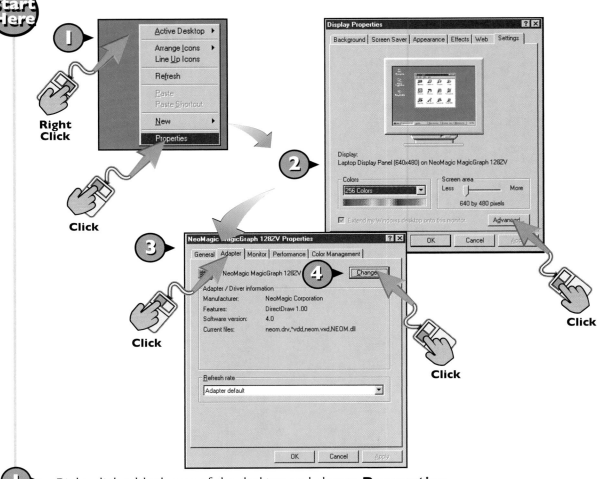

Start Here

Right Click

Click

Click

Click

Click

Click

✓ Your display is controlled by the display adapter (a card inside the system unit) and the monitor itself. Check the settings for both.

1 ▶ Right-click a blank area of the desktop and choose **Properties**.

2 ▶ In the **Settings** tab of the **Display Properties** dialog box, click the **Advanced** button.

3 ▶ Click the **Adapter** tab and make sure Windows is set up to use the correct display adapter.

4 ▶ If the display adapter is incorrect, click the **Change** button and follow instructions to choose the correct adapter.

Next Step

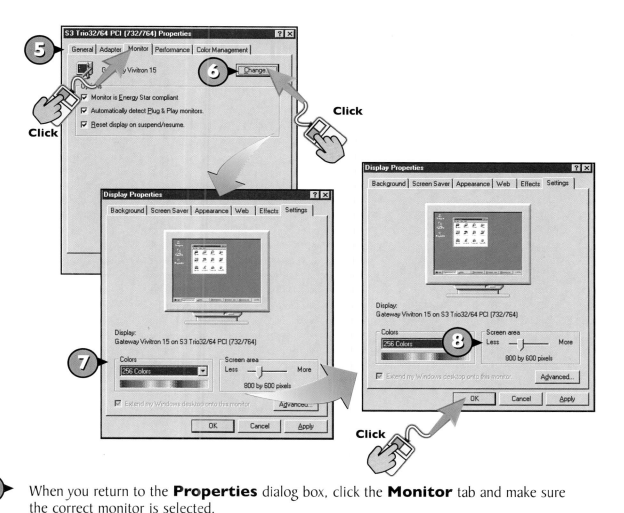

Click

Click

Click

5 When you return to the **Properties** dialog box, click the **Monitor** tab and make sure the correct monitor is selected.

6 If the wrong monitor is displayed, click the **Change** button and follow instructions to choose the correct monitor.

7 When you return to the **Display Properties** dialog box, make sure **Colors** is set to **256** or higher.

8 Make sure **Screen area** is set to **800 by 600** or higher and click **OK**.

✔ Graphics will appear grainy if **Colors** is set to less than **256** or if the **Screen area** is less than **800 by 600**.

✔ If you have trouble reading icon names in 800 by 600, open the **Display Properties** dialog box, click the **Settings** tab, click **Advanced**, and set the font size to **Large Fonts**.

End Task

If you don't have an icon for
your **CD-ROM** drive in My
Computer, first make sure
the cables, including the
power cable, are securely
connected. Check your
computer's **BIOS** settings,
as explained in Part 1, Tasks
17–22, to make sure your
computer is set up to
recognize the drive. Then,
try reinstalling the CD-
ROM driver, as shown here.

Task 10: Troubleshooting CD-ROM Drive Problems

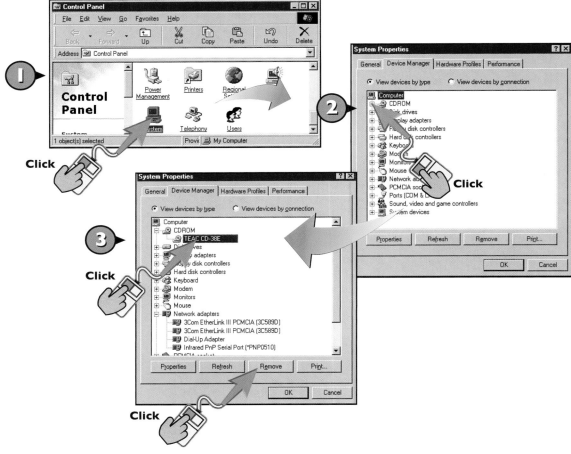

Open the Windows Control Panel and click the **System** icon.

In the **Device Manager** tab of the **System Properties** dialog box, click the plus sign next to **CD-ROM**.

Click the name of the CD-ROM driver to select it, and then click the **Remove** button.

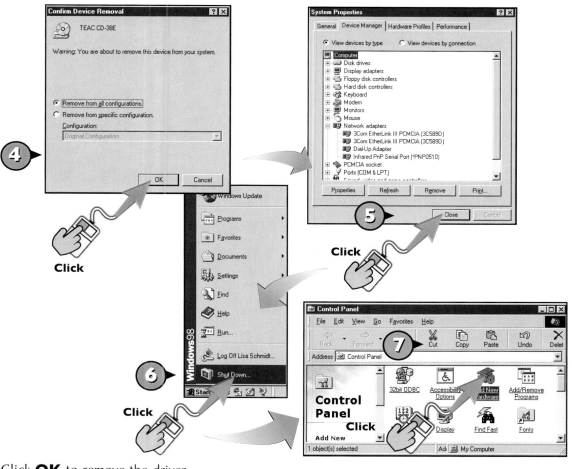

4 ▶ Click **OK** to remove the driver.

5 ▶ When you return to the **System Properties** dialog box, click **Close** to save your changes.

6 ▶ Shut down and restart Windows.

7 ▶ From the Windows Control Panel, run the Add New Hardware wizard and follow instructions to install the driver.

 If the problem persists, contact the **CD-ROM drive manufacturer** to determine whether an updated **CD-ROM driver** is available.

Task 11 : Correcting Printer Problems

If your printer won't print, first make sure the printer is plugged in and turned on and that the Online light is lit (not blinking). If your printer has panels or doors, make sure they are all closed. If the problem persists, check your printer settings, as shown here.

✓ Most printers have a self-test feature to help you make sure the problem is not with the printer itself. Check your printer's documentation.

✓ In step 4, check the back of the system unit to determine the printer port, typically the parallel printer port (LPT1). It should be marked with a printer icon. Some printers connect to the serial (COM) port, but that's rare.

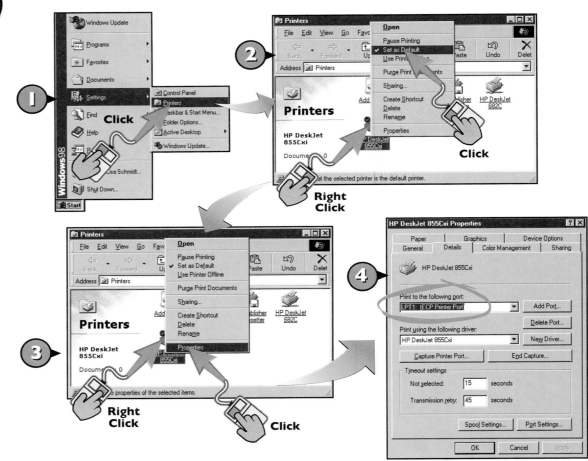

① Click **Start**, **Settings**, **Printers**.

② Right-click the icon for your printer and make sure there is a check mark next to **Set as Default**.

③ Right-click the printer icon and click **Properties**.

④ Click the **Details** tab and make sure the correct printer port is selected under **Print to the following port** (typically LPT1).

Next Step

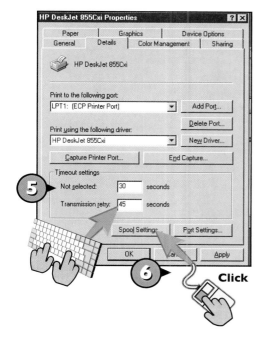

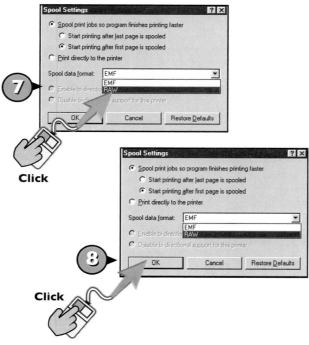

If you have an older printer, the driver that came with it might not work well in Windows 98. You may have better luck using a printer driver that came with Windows 98.

Click

Click

Click

5 ▸ Increase the numbers in the **Timeout settings** area so Windows will try longer to print a document before giving up.

6 ▸ If the printing problems persist, click the **Spool Settings** button.

7 ▸ Open the **Spool data format** drop-down list and click **RAW**.

8 ▸ Click **OK** to return to the **Properties** dialog box, and then click **OK** again.

✓ If the timeout settings are set too low, Windows will display an error message before the printer has a chance to print.

Task 12 : Troubleshooting Internet Problems

Although Microsoft's Internet Connection wizard can lead you through the process of creating an icon for connecting to the Internet, its default settings may be incorrect for your service provider. This task shows you how to check the settings.

 Start Here

Click

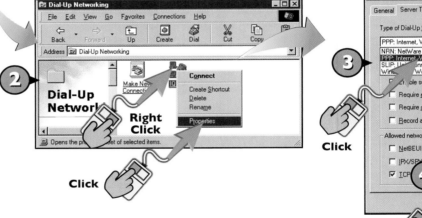

Right Click

Click

Click

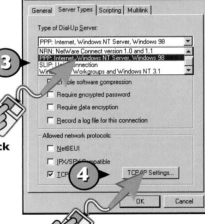

Click

Click

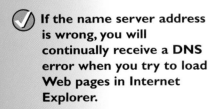 If the name server address is wrong, you will continually receive a DNS error when you try to load Web pages in Internet Explorer.

 In My Computer, click the **Dial-Up Networking** icon.

 Right-click the icon for your Internet service and click **Properties**.

 On the **Server Types** tab, open the **Type of Dial-Up Server** drop-down list and choose the type of Internet service you have.

 Click the **TCP/IP Settings** button.

 Next Step

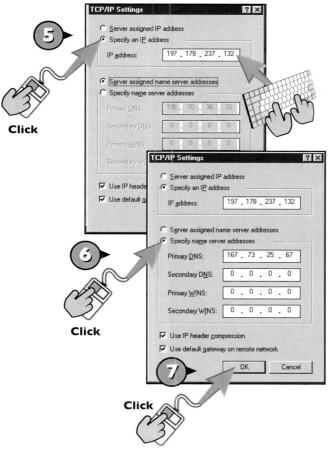

Click

Click

Click

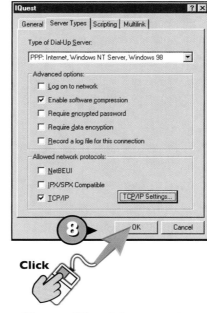

Click

> Because the Internet is constantly under construction, you should expect to encounter problems, most of which are out of your control.

> When wandering the Web, be flexible, yet persistent. You may have to try entering an address a couple times if the site is too busy to handle your request.

5 ▸ If your service provider assigned you an IP address, click **Specify an IP address** and type the address.

6 ▸ If your service provider told you to use a specific DNS address, click **Specify name server addresses** and type the address(es).

7 ▸ Click **OK** to save your changes and to close the **TCP/IP Settings** dialog box.

8 ▸ Click **OK** to save your settings and close the **Properties** dialog box.

Over the years, computers have become more and more complex, making it difficult not only to troubleshoot problems but also to keep track of what's installed on your system. The new Windows System Information utility addresses both of these issues, as shown here.

Task 13: Using the System Information Utility

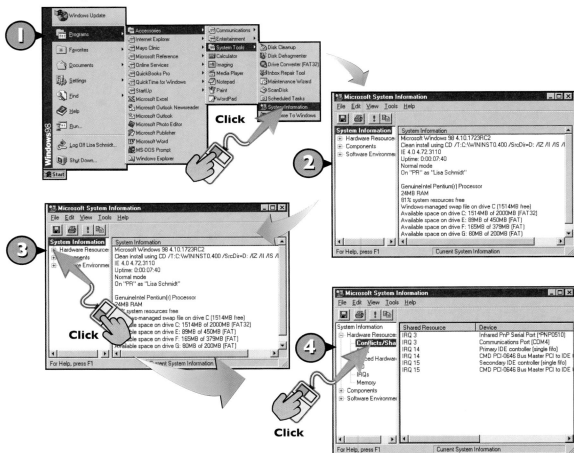

✓ System Information can help when you are discussing a problem with a technical support person.

Ⅰ▶ Click **Start**, **Programs**, **Accessories**, **System Tools**, **System Information**.

2▶ The opening screen displays general information about your computer's processor, memory, and available disk space.

3▶ To view more detailed information, click the plus sign next to the desired category.

4▶ Click the item for which you want to view additional details.

Next Step ▶

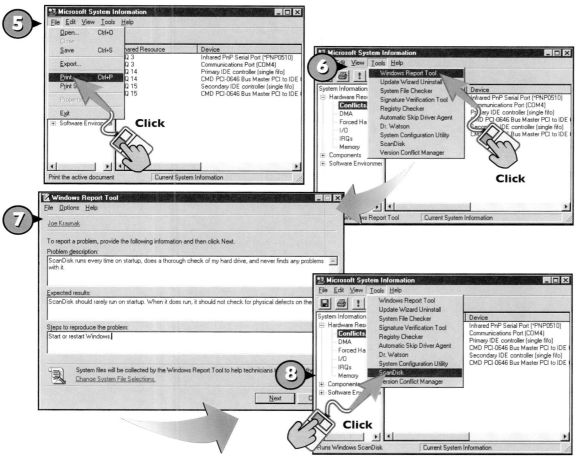

5 ▸ To print the information for future reference, open the **File** menu and choose **Print**.

6 ▸ For additional information and troubleshooting tools, open the **Tools** menu and select the desired option.

7 ▸ The Windows Report Tool allows you to report a problem to Microsoft and request specific help.

8 ▸ You can run ScanDisk right from the **System Information** window by selecting it from the **Tools** menu.

✅ **If you are requesting technical support via email, use File, Export to save the information as a text file and then send the file as an email attachment.**

The Windows Registry contains all of the settings that tell Windows how to perform its job, run installed applications, and use the components and devices that make up your computer. If this file is damaged, you may encounter serious problems. The Registry Checker can help your system recover when the Registry is damaged.

Task 14: Running the Windows Registry Checker

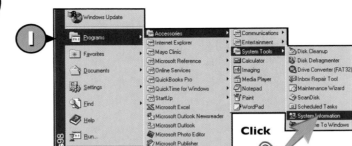

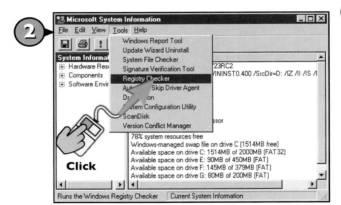

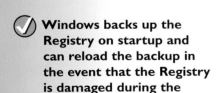

Windows backs up the Registry on startup and can reload the backup in the event that the Registry is damaged during the current session.

1. Click **Start**, **Programs**, **Accessories**, **System Tools**, **System Information**.

2. Open the **Tools** menu and click **Registry Checker**.

3. If no problems are found, Registry Checker asks if you want to back up the Registry. Click **Yes**.

4. When the **Backup Complete** dialog box appears, click **OK**.

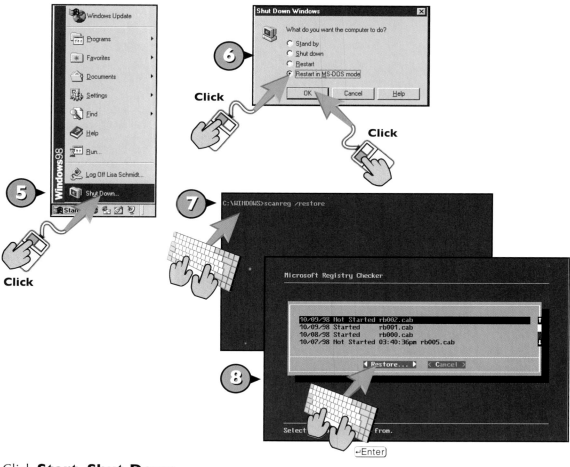

If the **Registry** is damaged, **Windows** typically loads the backup **Registry** when you start your computer. However, **Windows** doesn't always realize when the **Registry** is damaged. If you start your computer and encounter serious errors, you may need to force **Windows** to restore the **Registry**, as shown here.

Click **Start**, **Shut Down**.

Click **Restart in MS-DOS mode** and click **OK**.

At the DOS prompt, type `scanreg /restore` and press **Enter**.

Choose the Registry backup marked with a date indicating the last time Windows successfully started, and press **Enter**.

⚠ WARNING
The restored Registry will not contain settings for programs or devices you recently installed. You may need to reinstall programs or drivers.

Task 15: Editing the Windows Registry

The Windows Registry is the one of the most important files on your computer. Don't edit it unless a technical support person gives you a specific setting you need to change or enter. If you need to edit the Registry, this task shows you the basics.

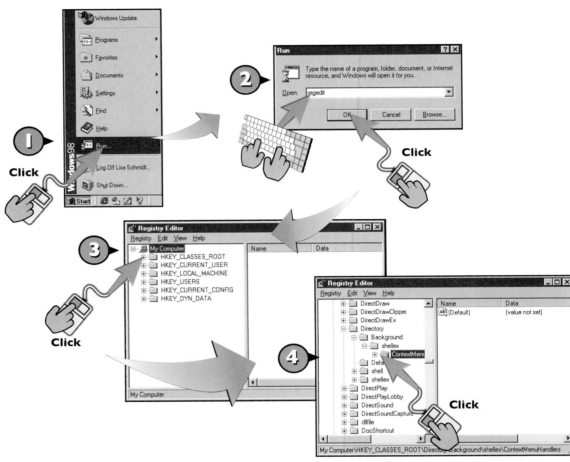

WARNING

Make a backup of the Registry, as explained in the previous task, before editing it.

1 ▶ Open the **Start** menu and click **Run**.

2 ▶ Type **regedit** and click **OK**.

3 ▶ Click the plus sign next to the **HKEY** folder in which you want to enter your change.

4 ▶ Continue expanding the list and then click the desired folder.

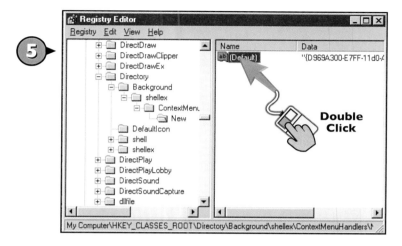

The Registry consists of folders, keys, and values. A *key* is a group of settings or values. In most cases, you will change existing values, as shown here, but you can add keys or values by choosing the desired option from the **Edit, New** menu.

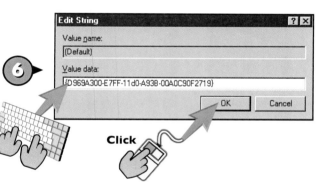

5 To change a value, double-click it in the list on the right.

6 Enter your changes and click the **OK** button.

⚠ **WARNING**
Before you change a value, write down the current value so you can change it back if needed.

Task 16: Running the System File Checker

In addition to the Registry, Windows loads several other system files on startup. If these files are damaged, you may encounter problems running Windows or your programs or using a device. You can use System File Checker to check, back up, and restore these system files.

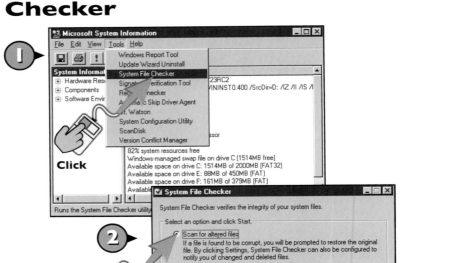

Click

Click

Click

Click

For a more thorough check, you can click the **Settings** button in the opening **System File Checker** dialog box and enter your preferences.

1. In the **System Information** window, open the **Tools** menu and choose **System File Checker**.

2. Make sure **Scan for altered files** is checked.

3. Click the **Start** button.

4. When System File Checker is finished, click the **Details** button.

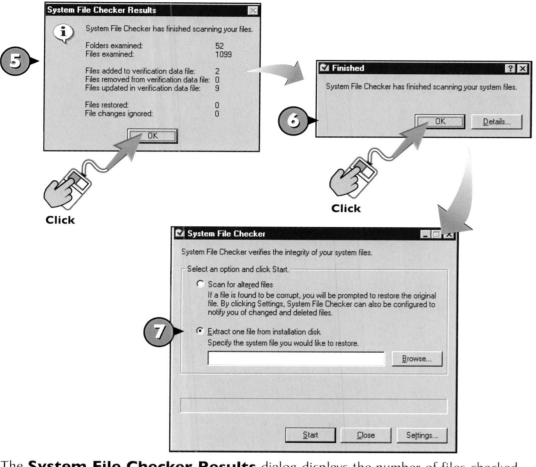

Click

Click

5 The **System File Checker Results** dialog displays the number of files checked, added to the verification data file, and restored. Click **OK**.

6 Click **OK** to return to System File Checker.

7 You can also use System File Checker to extract a single file from the Windows CD and place it in a folder on your hard disk.

⚠ WARNING
When extracting files from the Windows CD to your hard disk, copy the original file to a separate folder before replacing it.

Nearly every computer hardware and software company has its own Web site, where you can purchase products directly and find technical support for products you own. In addition, hardware manufacturers commonly post updated device drivers on their Web sites.

Task 17: Getting Technical Assistance on the Web

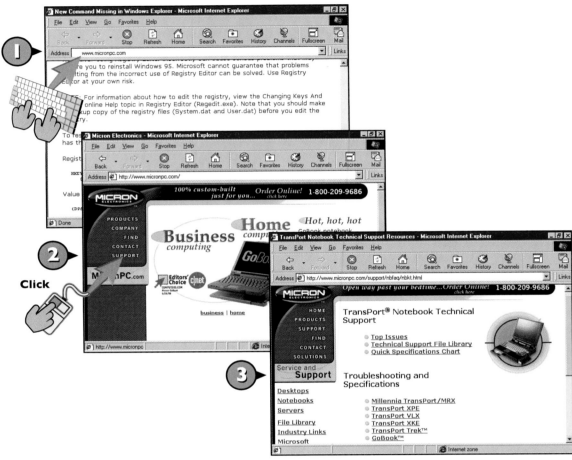

Click

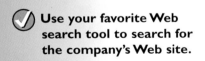 Use your favorite Web search tool to search for the company's Web site.

1 In Internet Explorer's **Address** text box, type the address of the company's Web site and press **Enter**.

2 Internet Explorer loads the page. Click the **Support** link or its equivalent.

3 Follow the trail of links to the specific product you own. When you see a link for the product, click it.

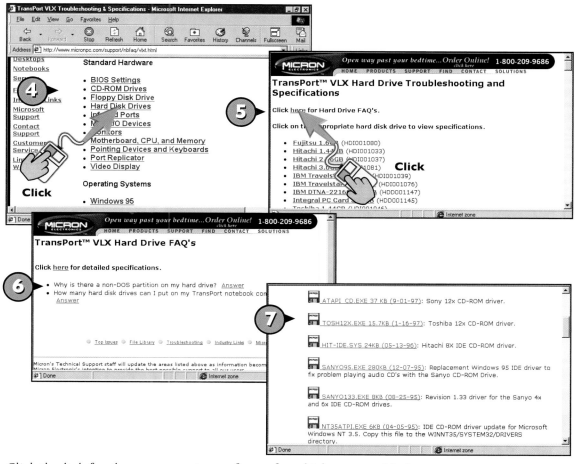

4️⃣ Click the link for the component or software for which you need help.

5️⃣ If the site has a FAQ (frequently asked questions) link, click the link to view a list of commonly asked questions.

6️⃣ The FAQ list appears, displaying questions and answers. You might have to click a link to view an answer.

7️⃣ If the site offers an updated device driver, click the link for downloading the driver and save the driver file.

✅ **For help from other users, go to www.lycos.com and search the message boards for your problem.**

✅ **To obtain help with Windows, click Start, Help, and then click the Web Help button in the Windows Help window.**

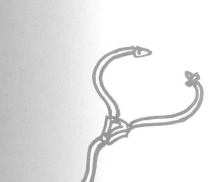

Task 18: Using Dr. Watson to Troubleshoot

Windows comes with a utility called Dr. Watson that won't help *you* much, but can help a technical support person track down the cause of a particular problem. Dr. Watson keeps track of all computer activity and logs all error messages and system problems.

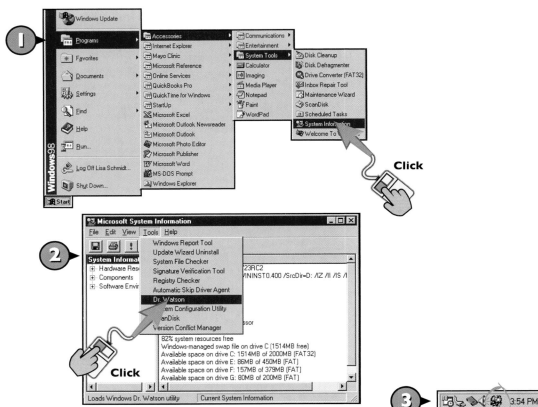

Start Here

Click

Click

Choose **Start**, **Programs**, **Accessories**, **System Tools**, **System Information**.

Open the **Tools** menu and choose **Dr. Watson**.

This runs Dr. Watson and displays an icon for Dr. Watson in the taskbar's system tray.

Next Step

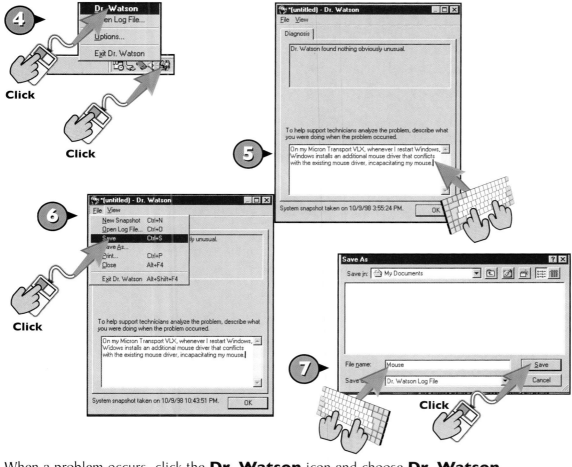

Dr. Watson logs activity as you perform tasks. When Windows displays an error message or locks up, Dr. Watson records the problem. You can then send Dr. Watson's log to a technical support person to provide the information needed to troubleshoot the problem.

4 When a problem occurs, click the **Dr. Watson** icon and choose **Dr. Watson**.

5 Type a detailed description of the problem.

6 Click **File, Save**.

7 Type a name for the file and click **Save**.

To print the log for your own reference, choose **File, Print**.

Keyboard Shortcuts

You can save time in Windows 98 by mastering a few keyboard shortcuts. The following table lists keystroke alternatives for common mouse moves.

Windows 98 Keyboard Shortcuts

Press | **To**

In My Computer and Windows Explorer

`Alt`+`←`	Move back to the previous view or folder.
`Alt`+`→`	Move ahead to the next view if you backed up.
`←Backspace`	Move up one level in the folder list.

In My Computer, Windows Explorer, and the Desktop

`Ctrl`+`Esc`	Open the **Start** menu. You can then press `↓` to highlight options on the menu and `→` to open the submenu for the current selection.
`Alt`+`Tab↹`	Change to the desired program when you have more than one program running. Pressing `Alt`+`Tab↹` once changes to the previous program. Holding down `Alt` and pressing `Tab↹` repeatedly lets you choose from a list of running programs.
`Ctrl`+**drag**	Copy a file.
`Ctrl`+`←Shift`+**drag**	Create a shortcut to a file or program.
`←Shift`+`Del`	Delete selected file(s) or folder(s) without using the Recycle Bin.
`F3`	Search for a file or folder.
`F5`	Refresh window contents.

`Ctrl`+`A`	Select all items on the desktop or in the current folder.
`Alt`+`↵Enter`	Display the properties of a selected object.
`←Shift`	Bypass AutoPlay while inserting an AutoPlay CD-ROM.

In Windows Explorer

`←`	Collapse an expanded folder or select the parent folder.
`→`	Expand a folder that has subfolders or select the next subfolder.
`Num Lock`+`-`	Collapse the selected, expanded folder.
`Num Lock`+`+`	Expand the selected folder.
`Num Lock`+`*`	Expand all folders that are below the selected subfolder.
`F6`	Toggle between left and right panes.

In Windows Dialog Boxes

`Ctrl`+`Tab↹`	Flip forward through tabs.
`Ctrl`+`←Shift`+`Tab↹`	Flip back through tabs.
`Tab↹`	Move from one option to another.
`←Shift`+`Tab↹`	Move back from one option to another.
`Spacebar`	Press the highlighted button, set or clear the highlighted check box, or select the highlighted option button.
`Esc`	Cancel and close the current dialog box.
`Alt`+**hotkey**	Select or deselect the option with the underlined letter.

⌐Enter	Press the highlighted button.
⌐Backspace	Move up one level in the folder tree in the **Save As** or **Open** dialog box.
F1	Display help for the currently selected option.
F4	Open the **Save In** or **Look In** list in the **Save As** or **Open** dialog box.
F5	Refresh the file and folder list in the **Save As** or **Open** dialog box.

In Windows Programs

F10	Activate the menu bar. You can then press ↓ to open the selected menu and press ← or → to change from one menu to another.
Alt+hotkey	Open the menu with the corresponding underlined letter.
hotkey	Choose the option with the corresponding underlined letter on the open menu.
⌐Shift+F10	Display the context menu for the selected text or object.
Esc	Close the open menu.
Alt+Spacebar	Open the current program window's system menu (to maximize, minimize, move, or resize the window).
Alt+-	Open the current document window's system menu (to maximize, minimize, move, or resize the window).
Ctrl+F4	Close the current document window.

Alt+F4	Close or exit the current program.
Ctrl+C	Copy the highlighted text or object and place it on the Windows Clipboard.
Ctrl+X	Remove the highlighted text or object and place it on the Windows Clipboard.
Ctrl+V	Insert (paste) the contents of the Windows Clipboard into the current document at the insertion point.
Ctrl+Z	Undo the previous action.
Del	Delete the selected text or object.
F1	Display help for the program.

Shortcuts with the Windows Logo Key

⊞	Open the **Start** menu.
⊞+Tab	Open the **Task Manager** dialog box.
⊞+F	Search for a file.
Ctrl+⊞+F	Search for a computer on your network.
⊞+F1	Display help.
⊞+R	Enter the **Start**, **Run** command.
⊞+Break	Display the **System Properties** dialog box.
⊞+E	Open the **My Computer** window.
⊞+D	Minimize all windows.
⌐Shift+⊞+M	Restore windows that you minimized.

A

Active Desktop   The new Windows work area that allows you to single-click icons to run programs and open documents. The Active Desktop can also display contents from Web pages.

Active Desktop component A frame on the Windows desktop that can automatically download updated content from the Web. Desktop components are commonly used to display news tickers, weather maps, and other ever-changing data on the desktop.

ActiveX   A relatively new technology that allows programs to share computer code, making programs and documents (especially Web pages) more dynamic.

address   On the Internet, a string of characters that specifies the location of a Web page, a person's mailbox, or a server.

address book   An electronic record book that helps you keep track of people's names, addresses, email addresses, and phone numbers. Address books are commonly used in email programs, such as Outlook Express, to enter complex email messages without typing them.

AutoDial   A Windows feature that automatically dials out with your modem when you perform a task that requires a connection to the Internet.

AutoHide   A taskbar feature that tucks the taskbar out of the way when you are working in a window or on the desktop.

AutoPlay   A CD-ROM feature that automatically starts to play a CD, when you insert it in the CD-ROM drive.

B

bi-directional printing   A feature supported by most new printers that establishes two-way communications between your computer and printer. A bi-directional printer can print 10 times faster than older printers.

BIOS   Pronounced "BUY-ose," short for *Basic Input/Output System*, it is the built-in set of instructions that tell the computer how to control the disk drives, keyboard, printer port, and other components that make up your computer.

BNC   Short for British Naval Connector, a cable commonly used for network connections. The cable is

similar to the type of cable used to connect a VCR to a TV set.

boot   To start a computer. When the computer starts, it reads a set of instructions that tell it how to operate.

Briefcase   A Windows feature that allows you to quickly and safely transfer documents from one PC to another (typically from a desktop to a notebook PC and vice versa), so you can take the documents home or on trips.

browse   To open Web pages and skip from one Web page to another by clicking hyperlinks.

C

Channel bar   A Windows tool that allows you to quickly open Web pages by clicking buttons. The Channel bar acts like a remote channel changer for a TV set.

client   A computer that requests data from another computer on the Internet or on a network. On the Internet, your computer is the client, and the computer from which you request Web pages is the server.

client/server network   A networking scheme in which the client computers are connected to a central computer (server) that does most of the work. The client computers may consist of little more than a keyboard, mouse, monitor, and connection to the server.

compact   To reduce the size of files so they take up less room and can travel across phone lines or network connections more quickly. Think of compacting as folding up a piece of paper.

Content Advisor   The censoring feature in Internet Explorer. Content Advisor blocks access to Web sites that contain undesirable material, including sex, violence, and offensive language.

cookie   Computer code that a Web site sends you to help keep track of your activity at that site. A cookie may contain the date you last visited the site or it can act as a tool that keeps track of the items you ordered at the site.

D

desktop   The Windows work surface. The desktop contains icons for running the programs you use most often. It also contains the Start button, taskbar, and Channel bar.

desktop theme   A new Windows feature that allows you to change the overall appearance and behavior of Windows. A desktop theme specifies the background, mouse pointer appearance, sounds, and screen saver that Windows is to use. For example, the Jungle scheme uses a lush, jungle background with mouse pointers that look like animals you might find in a jungle.

device driver   Software that tells Windows how to use a particular device that's connected to your computer, such as the monitor, mouse, printer, or modem.

Dial-Up Networking   A Windows feature that allows you to connect your computer to another computer on the Internet, a network, via modem, or using a special data cable.

Direct Cable Connection   A Windows feature that works with Dial-Up Networking to allow you to connect two computers using a special data cable.

Disk Cleanup   A Windows feature that automatically finds and deletes temporary files and uninstalls programs to provide more storage space on your hard disk.

docking station   A device for notebook PCs that increases the capabilities of the PC. A docking station typically allows you to connect the notebook PC to a full-size monitor and keyboard, a printer, a mouse, and an enhanced audio system.

download   To copy files from a remote computer to your computer. You can download files from the Web or from special FTP servers on the Internet.

Dr. Watson   A troubleshooting tool included with Windows 98. Dr. Watson logs your computer's activity as you work. When your system locks up, Dr. Watson records your system settings and any errors that occurred, so you can send the log to a technical support person to obtain specific help.

drag and drop   To use the mouse to drag an object from one place to another. To drop the object, you release the mouse button.

driver   See *device driver*.

E

ECP Short for *extended capabilities port*, a parallel port standard that allows bi-directional communications between the system unit and the printer. See also *bi-directional printing*.

email Short for *electronic mail*, an Internet and network communications tool that allows you to exchange messages with other users.

F

FAT32 A fairly recent hard disk innovation that divides large hard disk drives into small storage units, so the drive wastes less space. FAT is short for *file allocation table*, a seating chart that tells your computer where files are stored on a disk drive.

favorite A Web site that you add to a menu so you can quickly return to that site later. Internet Explorer allows you to mark Web sites as favorites.

file association A link between a program installed on your computer and the types of files it can open. When you install a program, it typically sets up a file association so you can open a file from My Computer, Windows Explorer, or from a Web page by clicking the file's link.

font A type style. When you format text, you typically change the font, type size, and color, and add enhancements, such as bold and italic.

FrontPage Express A program included with Windows 98 that you can use to create and edit Web pages.

FTP Short for *file transfer protocol*, a set of rules that governs the transfer of data across Internet connections. You can download files from Web and FTP sites by using Internet Explorer as your FTP program.

H

hardware profile A collection of settings that tell Windows which devices to use. Hardware profiles are typically used on notebook PCs to tell Windows if the PC is connected to a docking station that uses a different set of devices.

history list A list of addresses that Internet Explorer automatically records as you skip from one page to another on the Web. The history list allows you to quickly return to a site you have already visited.

home page 1. The first page Internet Explorer opens when you run it. 2. The first page a Web site displays when you connect to that site.

HTML Short for *hypertext markup language*, a set of codes used to format Web pages. These codes control the appearance of text, insert graphics and audio clips, insert tables, and much more.

HTML layer On the Windows desktop, the portion of the desktop that displays the Channel bar, Active Desktop components, and other Web content. The Windows desktop contains two layers: the HTML layer and the icon layer. See also *icon layer*.

hub A network device that contains jacks (similar to phone jacks). To network computers, you connect a cable from the network card on each computer to the central hub.

hyperlink Highlighted text, a graphic, or another object that points to another document. On the Web, you click hyperlinks to jump from one page to another.

I

icon layer On the Windows desktop, the portion of the desktop that displays the icons you click. See also *HTML layer*.

IMAP Short for *Internet Message Access Protocol*, a set of rules that control the way you receive email messages on the Internet. IMAP is similar, but more powerful, than the more common POP standard. See also *POP*.

Inbox Assistant A tool in Outlook Express that can automatically route incoming mail to specified folders based on the name of the person who sent the message or on the description of the message.

infrared A technology that supports wireless connections, commonly used for connecting a computer to a network,

printer, mouse, or keyboard. Infrared communications use a similar technology as that used for TV remote controls.

Internet A group of computers all over the world that are connected to each other. Using your computer and a modem, you can connect to these other computers and tap their resources. You can view pictures, listen to sounds, watch video clips, play games, chat with other people, and even shop.

Internet Explorer Microsoft's Web browser, included with Windows 98. You use Internet Explorer to open and display pages on the World Wide Web.

intranet A network that is set up to look and act like the Internet but does not allow outsiders to access it. More and more companies are setting up their networks as intranets to simplify navigation.

IPX/SPX Short for *Internetwork Packet EXchange/Sequenced Packet EXchange*, a network protocol especially useful for playing multi-player computer games over a network connection.

IRdA Short for InfraRed Data Association, a group of manufacturers who specialize in designing and making infrared devices. See also *infrared*.

L

link See *hyperlink*.

log off To disconnect from the Internet or a network.

log on To connect to the Internet or a network by entering your username and password.

LPT An acronym used to specify a printer port. This acronym initially stood for *line printer terminal*, but is now used more generically for any type of printer.

M

mail filter A screening tool that routes incoming email messages to special folders based on the name of the sender or the message description. See also *Inbox Assistant*.

mail server   A computer that's set up to enable email message transfers over the Internet or on a network.

Maintenance wizard   A Windows 98 tool that can automatically perform several system maintenance tasks (including scanning your disks for errors and deleting temporary files) at a scheduled time.

map drive   On a network, to enter settings that make a disk drive on another computer look and act as though the drive is on your computer. When you map a drive to your computer, it appears in the Save and Open dialog boxes in your applications.

modem   A device that can connect your computer to the Internet, a commercial online service, or any other computer over the phone lines. Modem is short for *MOdulator/DEModulator*.

N

NetBEUI   Short for *NetBios Enhanced User Interface*, a protocol that is used for fast data transfers over a network. See also *network protocol*.

Network Neighborhood   A Windows 98 tool that displays all available network resources, including shared disk drives and printers.

network protocol   A set of rules that governs the transfer of data on a network.

news server   A computer that's set up to allow users to post messages and replies and read messages.

newsgroup   An area on the Internet where users can read and post messages and reply to messages. Think of a newsgroup as an electronic bulletin board.

O

offline   Disconnected. On the Internet, if you incur charges based on the time you are connected, you can use special tools built into Internet Explorer and Outlook Express to retrieve data and then read or use the data offline.

Outlook Express   The email/newsgroup program included with Windows 98.

P

PC card   A credit-card-sized add-on, typically used in notebook PCs. A PC card may be used to add memory, a network card, a modem, or another disk drive to your notebook PC without having to open the PC to install the device.

PCMCIA   Short for *Personal Computer Memory Card International Association*, an organization that has set standards for notebook computer expansion cards. See also *PC card*.

peer-to-peer network   A networking scheme in which the networked computers are connected to one another rather than to a central computer (as on a *client/server network*). On a peer-to-peer network, each computer acts as both a client and a server. See also *client* and *server*.

Personal Web Server   A Windows 98 tool that allows you to set up your computer as a Web server. This is useful for testing Web pages before placing them on the Web and for using your computer as a Web server on a peer-to-peer network.

POP   Short for *Post Office Protocol*, a set of rules that governs the transfer of email messages across the Internet.

port   An outlet on a computer into which you can plug devices, such as a mouse, keyboard, monitor, or printer.

port replicator   See *docking station*.

power-management utility
A power-saving tool that can automatically shut down power to devices, such as your hard disk drive and monitor, when the computer is not in use.

protocol   A collection of rules that govern the transfer of data, typically over the Internet or on a network.

Q

Quick Launch toolbar   A new Windows 98 toolbar that's embedded in the taskbar. The Quick Launch toolbar provides single-click access to Internet Explorer, Outlook Express, Channels, and the Windows desktop.

Quick View   A Windows feature that allows you to preview a document file before opening it. To use Quick View, you right-click the document's icon and choose **Quick View**.

R

read-ahead buffer   A temporary storage area that increases the speed of a device, such as a disk drive or CD-ROM drive. Your computer can read more information from the disk than is immediately needed, store that data in RAM, and then quickly access it when it is needed.

read-only access   A security feature that allows a person to use a disk, folder, or file, but does not allow the user to change it. On the Internet and on networks, read-only access prevents unauthorized users from damaging files.

Recycle Bin   A temporary holding area for deleted files. Whenever you delete a file, it is placed in the Recycle Bin. Until you empty the Recycle Bin, you can recover files from it.

Registry   A Windows file that includes settings and preferences for your system's applications and hardware. The Windows Registry is one of the most important files on your computer. If it is damaged, Windows may not be able to start or may not operate properly.

Registry Checker   A Windows 98 tool that automatically checks and optionally backs up the Windows Registry. See also *Registry*.

S

scrap   Copied or cut data that is stored as an icon on the Windows desktop. You can use scraps to quickly paste data into other documents by dragging and dropping the scrap icon from the Windows desktop into the document.

security zone   An area on the Internet for which Internet Explorer has specific instructions on the type of activities to allow. There are four security zones: Local (intranet), Trusted (for sites you trust), Restricted (for sites you don't trust), and Internet (for all other sites).

server On a network or the Internet, the computer from which you request data. For instance, you connect to a Web server to request Web pages. You connect to a mail server to retrieve email messages.

shortcut A copy of an icon that points to another object on your computer or on a network. Shortcuts allow you to quickly access disks, folders, files, and programs.

spool To print a document to your hard disk and have the print data fed to your printer as the printer is ready to receive it. Spooling allows a program to quickly finish printing a document so you can perform other tasks while the document prints in the background.

subscription An object that you set up on your computer to automatically download updated pages and other content from the Web.

System Information utility A Windows tool that displays information about your computer, including the amount of memory installed and the amount of disk space available. The System Information utility also allows you to run other utilities for checking your system files and running ScanDisk.

system tray An area on the right end of the taskbar that displays the current time and icons for programs that are running in the background.

T

T-connector A network cable connector that allows you to connect your computer to two other computers on a network.

Task Scheduler A Windows tool that allows you to set up programs to run at specific times. This is useful for setting up your computer to automatically back up files or scan your disk drives for errors.

taskbar A bar at the bottom of the Windows desktop that contains the Start button, Quick Launch toolbar, system tray, and buttons for programs that are currently running. You can quickly switch to a program by clicking its button in the taskbar.

TCP/IP Short for *Transmission Control Protocol/Internet Protocol*, a collection of rules that governs the transfer of data over the Internet.

terminator A cap that fits over one end of a T-connector on a network card. If you connect your computer to only one other computer on a network using BNC cables, you must cap the open end of the T-connector with a terminator.

troubleshooter A tool accessible from the Windows Help system that asks a series of questions to help you track down the cause of a common hardware problem.

U-V

upload To copy a folder or file from your computer to a remote computer, typically over an Internet connection.

virtual memory Disk space that your system uses as RAM (memory).

W

wallpaper A design that Windows displays as the desktop background instead of using a solid color.

Web Short for *World Wide Web*, a part of the Internet that consists of multimedia documents that are interconnected by links. To move from one document to another, you click on a link, which may appear as highlighted text or as a small picture or icon. The Web contains text, sound and video clips, pictures, catalogs, and much more.

Web page A document on the Internet that you open in Internet Explorer. Web pages can contain text, graphics, links to other pages, audio clips, animations, and much more.

Web Publishing wizard A series of dialog boxes that leads you step-by-step through the process of copying a Web document (and its associated files) from your computer to a Web server.

Web server A computer that's set up to deliver Web pages on request. Whenever you enter an address of a Web site or page in Internet Explorer, you connect to a Web server, which sends you the requested page.

Web style An option in My Computer that displays the contents of your disks and folders as they would appear on a Web page. In Web style, disk, folder, and file icons appear as links, giving you single-click access to resources.

Windows Update A new feature in Windows 98 that can download Windows updates and help you find and install updated device drivers on the Web. You'll find Windows Update at the top of the Start menu.

WinPopup A Windows networking application that allows you to send messages to other users on your network. When you send a message, it immediately pops up on the other user's screen.

cleaning mouse, 206-207
Client for Microsoft Networks, 144
clip art (Windows 98 CD), 28-29
colors on Web pages, modifying, 49
COM ports (modems), 200-201
commands
    Active Desktop menu, View As Web
        Page, 76
    File menu, Work Offline, 40-41
    Settings menu, Printers, 16-17
    Tools menu (Outlook), Accounts, 96-97
    View menu, Folder Options, 70, 74-77
components
    Active Desktop, adding from Web, 84-85
    fonts, removing, 20-21
    network
        Dial-Up Networking, 141
        Dial-Up Server, 141
        Direct Cable Connection, 141
        installing, 140-141
computers
    BIOS settings, adjusting, 30-31, 35
    direct cable connections, configuring,
        146-147
    Dr. Watson utility, 226-227
    hardware profiles, creating, 26-27
    power-management settings, 22-23
    power-saving options, 34
    Registry Checker, troubleshooting,
        218-219
    System Information utility,
        troubleshooting, 216-217
configuring
    direct cable connections between two
        computers, 146-147
    docking station for notebook PCs,
        120-121
    history settings (Internet Explorer), 48
    incoming messages (Outlook Express),
        103
    Internet connection settings, 214-215
    Internet Explorer options, 44
    intranets, 158-159

Maintenance wizard, 5
modems, 200-201
mouse properties, 206-207
multiple user settings, 24-25
network logon preferences, 148
Outlook Express, 58-59
    layout options, 94-95, 100
Recycle Bin, drive space settings, 8
security settings (Internet Explorer),
    50-51
temporary files (Internet Explorer),
    46-47
connecting
    Internet
        Dial-Up Networking, 56-57
        troubleshooting, 214-215
    newsgroups, 99
    peripherals, infrared connections,
        128-129
    to office PC via modem, 126-127
conserving
    battery power in notebook PCs,
        130-131
    disk space (Internet Explorer), 47
    power, 22-23, 34
Content Advisor (Internet Explorer),
    54-55
Control Panel
    desktop themes, selecting, 90-91
    modems, muting, 178
    multimedia audio settings, 203
    shortcuts, placing, 171
converting
    folders into toolbars, 83
    hard drives, FAT16 to FAT32 (Drive
        Converter), 10-11
    Web pages to wallpaper, 78
cookies, 53
copying files
    between notebook PCs and desktop
        PCs, 122-123
    to floppy disks (Send To folder), 176

creating
    desktop shortcuts, 170-171
    document scraps, 175
    Documents menu shortcut, 177
    email address book, 110-111
    file associations, 66-67
    hardware profiles, 26-27
    links in Web pages, 184-185
    message folders (Outlook Express), 108
    toolbars, 83
    Web pages (FrontPage Express),
        182-183
Crtl+A keystroke (selecting all
    objects), 166-167
Crtl+Alt+Delete keystroke (system
    lock-ups), 192-193
Crtl+Esc keystroke (Start menu
    display), 166-167
customizing
    background (My Computer), 188-189
    folders, 74-77

D

data, submitting over Web sites, 52-53
deactivating multimedia settings
    (Internet Explorer), 62-63
decreasing virtual memory, 15
default colors on Web pages,
    changing, 49
deferred printing, 132-133
defragmenting hard disks, 12
deleting
    email accounts, 97
    files from Recycle Bin, 8
    fonts, 21
    history settings (Internet Explorer), 48
    messages (Outlook Express), 106
    shortcuts, 163
    temporary files, 6
        Internet Explorer, 47

F

G - H

I

Internet Explorer

J - K

M